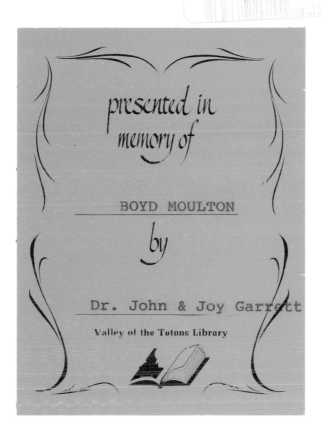

presented in memory of

BOYD MOULTON

by

Dr. John & Joy Garrett

Valley of the Tetons Library

WHEN YOU CAN'T DO IT ALONE

WHEN YOU CAN'T DO IT ALONE

BRENT L. TOP

DESERET
BOOK

SALT LAKE CITY, UTAH

© 2008 Brent L. Top

Library of Congress Cataloging-in-Publication Data

Top, Brent L.
    When you can't do it alone / Brent L. Top.
        p. cm.
    Includes bibliographical references and index.
    ISBN 978-1-59038-958-4 (hardcover : alk. paper)
    1. Top, Brent L.   2. Depressed persons—Religious life.   3. Spiritual life—Church of Jesus Christ of Latter-day Saints.   4. Depression, Mental—Religious aspects—Church of Jesus Christ of Latter-day Saints.   I. Title.
    BX8643.D44T67 2008
    289.3092—dc22
    [B]   2008019738

Printed in the United States of America
Publishers Printing, Salt Lake City, UT

10   9   8   7   6   5   4   3   2   1

CONTENTS

Preface vii

1   Help Thou Mine Unbelief 1

2   Think on Him 13

3   Thank Him 35

4   Serve Him 51

5   Learn of Him 71

6   Trust in Him 90

7   Hold On to Him 109

8   Strengthened by the Hand of the Lord 119

    Works Cited 135

    Index 139

However halting our steps are toward him—though they shouldn't be halting at all—his steps are never halting toward us. May we have enough faith to accept the goodness of God and the mercy of his Only Begotten Son. May we come unto him and his gospel and be healed. And may we do more to heal others in the process. When the storms of life make this difficult, may we still follow his bidding to "come," keeping our eye fixed on him forever and single to his glory. In doing so we too will walk triumphantly over the swelling waves of life's difficulties and remain unterrified amid any rising winds of despair.

—ELDER JEFFREY R. HOLLAND,
"Come unto Me," 23

PREFACE

THIS IS A VERY PERSONAL STORY. In fact, it is so personal that I have struggled with whether or not I should write about my experience. Obviously, I have decided to share with you my story, but let me tell you a few of the reasons for my reluctance.

First, the "natural man" in me fears that you will think less of me—that I lack faith, that I don't really understand (or believe) the principles I have spent my lifetime teaching, or that if I had a stronger testimony my experience would have been less painful. Self-disclosure is difficult.

Second, I hesitate to set myself up as an expert in anything or to assume a position of authority. I don't have all the answers for myself and my own family—let alone for others. My experiences are probably not exactly like yours. My struggles are not your struggles and my weaknesses are not your weaknesses (lucky for you!).

But there are similarities in our challenges because of our shared human condition and the desire instilled in us by the gospel to do better and to be better. We can learn from each other and help strengthen each other. In doing so, we seek to fulfill our covenants "to bear one another's burdens, that they may be light" (Mosiah 18:8) and "succor the weak, lift up the hands which hang down, and strengthen the feeble knees" (D&C 81:5). I am grateful for those who have succored and strengthened me when my burdens caused my knees to buckle.

I hope that in some small way the things I have learned will be a source of insight, inspiration, and strength to you—whatever your burdens, whatever your challenges, whatever your circumstances. Perhaps you already know these things, and I don't profess to teach you anything new. I have learned, however, that there is strength in always remembering the lessons we learn and continually applying them in the various seasons and circumstances of our lives.

Another reason why I am somewhat hesitant to be too open in this book is the profound sacredness that I feel in the Lord's tutoring of me. In my extremities He has cradled me. In my discouragement, He has buoyed me up. In those moments when I have been at a loss for explanations, He has given me understanding. At other times when I have been left without understanding—when I can see no "meaning in the madness," He has given me peace. You cannot experience these things without feeling a deep sense of reverence. I hope that my words will reflect that reverence.

Elder Orson F. Whitney observed:

> No pain that we suffer, no trial we experience is wasted. It ministers to our education, to the development of such qualities as patience, faith, fortitude and humility. All that we suffer and all that we endure, especially when we endure it patiently, builds up our characters, purifies our hearts, expands our souls, and makes us more charitable, more worthy to be called the children of God . . . and it is through sorrow and suffering, toil and tribulation, that we gain the education that we came here to acquire and which will make us more like our Father and

Mother in heaven (as quoted by Spencer W. Kimball in *Faith Precedes the Miracle*, 98).

The phrases "it ministers to our education" and "that we gain the education that we came here to acquire" jump out at me. Perhaps that is because I am a teacher. The longer I live and the more I experience in life, the more I learn that education is not merely learning new things, but living in a new way—a better way. Yet "the education that we came here to acquire" is more than just acquiring knowledge for ourselves to better our lives; it is for sharing with others and helping to better their lives. Each day I pass through the gates of Brigham Young University, where a sign reads "Enter to Learn. Go Forth to Serve." So it is with our own "educational" experiences of pain and problems and difficulties and discouragement. We "enter" them to learn what the Lord would have us learn, not just so we can endure more faithfully, but also so that we can "go forth to serve" others through lifting and loving.

Elder Neal A. Maxwell said that the Lord made known to him that his own struggle against cancer was designed to give "authenticity" to his ministry (see Bruce C. Hafen, *A Disciple's Life*, 562). In a much smaller way, I feel that, because of what I have experienced, I can testify "with authenticity" of the peace and strength that indeed come to those who cast their burdens upon the Lord. In a way that I never quite imagined before, I became a witness to the Lord's promise: "My grace is sufficient for thee: for my strength is made perfect in weakness" (2 Corinthians 12:9). I now have a better understanding of what Paul meant when he declared in the same verse: "Most gladly therefore will I rather glory in my infirmities, that the power of Christ may rest upon me."

As I have shared my experience with others I have noticed that some people are surprised (and maybe even a little uncomfortable) with my speaking so candidly about my own struggles. However, most have been grateful to discover that they are not alone in their own feelings. With shared experience can come shared hope and shared strength from learning from each other, by linking arms together and looking to the Lord as the ultimate source of our strength and comfort. It is to this end that I have written this book.

I, alone, am responsible for the ideas and applications presented in this book. They do not represent the official doctrine or position of The Church of Jesus Christ of Latter-day Saints, nor would I want anyone to assume that I am speaking for the leadership of the Church. I fully understand that the doctrine of the Church is declared only by the Lord's anointed prophets, seers, and revelators. I sustain them wholeheartedly. I have tried my best to ensure that the ideas presented here are in harmony with the teachings of the scriptures and leaders of the Church. If there are doctrinal deficiencies, they come strictly from my own weaknesses. It is my hope and prayer that this book will, in some small way, strengthen your love and gratitude for the Lord and increase your understanding of the enabling power of His grace.

1

HELP THOU MINE UNBELIEF

I AM A RELIGIOUS EDUCATOR by profession. For over thirty years, as a seminary and institute teacher and religion professor at BYU, I have dissected and discussed the scriptures. With each successive reading I glean new insights and fresh applications. Myriad are the things that I have learned through the years from my students and colleagues. Being a teacher is also being a student. Most of the time, I feel that I learn more than I teach. In addition, there have also been those moments of clarity when I am instructed "from on high" by the power of the Holy Ghost. The Prophet Joseph Smith described that revelatory experience as "pure intelligence flowing into you" and "sudden strokes of ideas" (*Teachings of the Prophet Joseph Smith,* 151). Each of these methods of learning is valuable. There is, however, another way that I have gained gospel understanding—a way that transcends, but links, all others. That is through personal experience.

I must admit that I have not always been a great fan of the personal experience method of learning. That probably stems from something I heard my father say to me on many occasions when I did something stupid: "That is the difference between youth and wisdom!" I later found a quote that I would throw back at my dad when he would gleefully say that to me: "The difference between youth and experience is that the young assume intelligence is a substitute for experience, while the old assume experience is a substitute for intelligence." Neither of us liked the other's quote. Now that I am getting older, I find myself appreciating experience (and losing intelligence) more and more.

True learning—life-changing learning—cannot be obtained without an immersion in the font of personal experience. I am not just talking about a kind of common sense that inevitably comes with personal experience or the education acquired in the "school of hard knocks," but a deeply spiritual linking of experience and intelligence, "or, in other words, light and truth" (D&C 93:36), that causes a person to see with new eyes, hear with new ears, and feel with a new heart.

There is a story from the life of the Savior that I have read many times and taught to hundreds of New Testament students. Yet I didn't fully understand it until I experienced it. It is the familiar story of Jesus walking on water. No—I didn't walk on water! But I did feel something akin to what Peter experienced.

> But the ship was now in the midst of the sea, tossed with waves: for the wind was contrary.
>
> And in the fourth watch of the night Jesus went unto them, walking on the sea.
>
> And when the disciples saw him walking on the sea, they were troubled, saying, It is a spirit; and they cried out for fear.
>
> But straightway Jesus spake unto them, saying, Be of good cheer; it is I; be not afraid.
>
> And Peter answered him and said, Lord, if it be thou, bid me come unto thee on the water.

And he said, Come. And when Peter was come down out of the ship, he walked on the water, to go to Jesus.

But when he saw the wind boisterous, he was afraid; and beginning to sink, he cried, saying, Lord, save me.

And immediately Jesus stretched forth his hand, and caught him, and said unto him, O thou of little faith, wherefore didst thou doubt?

And when they were come into the ship, the wind ceased.

Then they that were in the ship came and worshipped him, saying; Of a truth thou art the Son of God (Matthew 14:24–33).

For me, "stepping out of the boat" was when I was called to serve as a mission president. I had served in many different callings in the Church, but this was in many ways much different and far more difficult. It is exciting, but also extraordinarily humbling, to be interviewed by a member of the Quorum of the Twelve Apostles and to have the call extended by a member of the First Presidency. The months between receiving the call and entering the mission field, while busy with preparations, seemed kind of like we were living in a no-man's-land—we couldn't totally focus on home responsibilities (because we would be gone for three years), and we were not yet ready to assume mission responsibilities. It was like we didn't belong in either world. Even though I received materials to study, including the *Mission President's Handbook* and CDs of previous mission president training seminars to listen to and absorb, I still didn't know quite what to expect. I "picked the brains" of former mission presidents—soaking up all I could learn from them. Despite all this, it still seemed unreal. That feeling of "unrealness" (if there is such a word) didn't last long, however. Reality soon set in—big time.

Someone once told me that being a mission president is like being dropped out of an airplane onto the roof of a speeding bullet train filled with passengers. You have to run along the top of the train, maintaining your balance, fighting against the physical forces and unexpected twists and turns that could throw you off, make your way to the controls, take over as engineer, guide the "out-of-control" train safely into the station without even breaking into a sweat, and then stand on the station platform and pleasantly greet the departing passengers as if there was nothing to it.

I started to sense that a little when I was set apart by President Boyd K. Packer. I was so nervous, and still somewhat in the fog of unrealness, that I don't remember all that he said to me in my blessing. There was one statement, however, I will never forget. "I bless you that you will not panic," President Packer declared. That phrase was comforting, but it was the next phrase that was a little unnerving—"when you have reason to panic." I felt like the other shoe had just dropped!

Words cannot fully describe the sense of inadequacy that enveloped me as we participated in the new mission president training seminar at the Missionary Training Center. As I looked around the room at the other mission presidents and their wives, I felt like I didn't belong—that I was out of my league, that I was a struggling T-ball player and they were all-star major leaguers. They all beamed with competence and confidence. They seemed to be filled to the brim with spirituality and wisdom forged by their vast Church leadership experience. I felt just the opposite. I knew it was a remarkable privilege to serve as a mission president, but I was overwhelmed with feelings of self-doubt and fear that I would "mess up"—let the Lord, my family, my friends, and myself down. The more we were instructed concerning our responsibilities, the worse I felt.

I know the counsel given at the training seminar was not intended to discourage, but rather to instruct and prepare us. Yet, in my already overwhelmed mental condition, the counsel and direction just added more to the list of "gotta do's" and "oughta be's"—a growing list of tasks and traits that seemed impossible to master. The "mountain" I was expecting myself to climb was insurmountable. Instead of leaving the MTC spiritually invigorated and ready to take on the world—like Caleb in the Old Testament saying "give me this mountain" (Joshua 14:12)— I was ready to "shrink [and] shun the fight" ("True to the Faith," *Hymns*, no. 254).

Things got worse after we arrived in the mission field. There were the relentless responsibilities, with more to learn and do than I had time or energy for. There were the many problems that always needed addressing, the sleepless nights worrying about someone or something, the crazy pace of interviews and zone conferences and transfers and firesides and stake conferences—and phone calls. I got so that my heart skipped a beat each time the phone rang—"Now, what has gone wrong?" Sometimes I felt that being a mission president was like playing the Whack-a-Mole game at the arcade—you whack down one problem and immediately two more pop up. Instead of experiencing the joy the Lord has promised to those in His service, I felt bogged down, overburdened, and burned-out. I wasn't sure I would survive three years.

It was during a particularly difficult time that I had my Peter-like experience. I had responded to a call from the Master, like Peter had, and "stepped out of the boat." In a way, I was figuratively walking on water—trying to do what the Lord had asked me to do even though it seemed impossible. There had been those moments when it was clear to me that the mantle was far greater than the man. Miracles were occurring around me and within me. I had indeed seen the hand of the Lord helping me and the mission. I just didn't recognize and appreciate them as much as I should have. Like Peter, I got distracted and became frightened when I "saw the wind boisterous" (Matthew 14:30). Each problem I encountered and each responsibility I had to face became like fierce waves crashing against me, threatening to knock me over, sink me, and drown me in the depths of despair.

I don't know exactly what the catalyst was to my emotional and spiritual crash. I had felt it coming on for months. There had been some serious problems in the mission with which I had wrestled, draining my reservoirs of physical energy and mental strength. I felt spiritually spent. Another mission president seminar brought to the surface my feelings of inadequacy. Comparisons of our weaknesses with others' strengths always leave us feeling inadequate, overwhelmed, and like we can never measure up. "We aren't doubling our baptisms like the _____ Mission." "I should be more like President _____." "We are not doing all we should be doing." "I need to be better at that." "Why didn't I come up with good ideas like that?" My mind was filled with such self-defeating and service-limiting thoughts. The "gotta do's" and the "oughta be's" were again torturing me.

It finally all came crashing down on me early one Sunday morning. The cumulative weight of the problems in the mission, the frantic pace of my schedule, and the vexing feelings of fear and self-doubt all combined to literally knock me down and lay me low. I couldn't get out of bed. I shook uncontrollably. My heart was pounding. I couldn't stop crying. The thought of having to do one more thing or go to one more meeting or speak in one more setting filled me with a profound sense of dread or, as Alma described it, "inexpressible horror" (Alma 36:14). I thought I was going to die—literally.

Depression runs in my family. I have had bouts with it in the past, but I had never experienced anything like this before. I had heard about panic attacks, but I had never experienced them. This, however, was more than just a panic attack. It was a full-blown, flat-out depression and anxiety assault—a total breakdown. The pain I experienced was physical, mental, and spiritual—something akin to what Alma felt for his sins: "My soul was harrowed up to the greatest degree" (36:12);

"tormented with the pains of hell" (36:13); "racked with . . . torment" (36:12); "Oh, thought I, that I could be banished and become extinct both soul and body" (36:15).

What I was experiencing was a breakdown of confidence, a breakdown of hope, a breakdown of faith. It was not only a physical and emotional crisis for me, but a spiritual one as well. Just as Peter when the boisterous winds and waves overwhelmed him, I too was "sinking" and cried out, "Lord, save me" (Matthew 14:30). The Lord reached out to me, like He did with Peter, and "stretched forth his hand, and caught [me]" (Matthew 14:31). For me, however, the rescue wasn't immediate. Getting "back in the boat" took time. I had to learn how to grab hold of the outstretched hand of the Savior. I had to learn through personal experience how to allow Him to rescue me.

I wasn't immediately healed. My difficult circumstances were not immediately or miraculously transformed into a "bed of roses." What was immediate, however, was the help I received from my wife, Wendy. She had once been where I was and she knew how to help and what to say. As she cradled me in her arms, she infused faith into me. "Focus on Christ," she lovingly said to me. "Focus on His love for you. Focus on how He has carried you in the past. Focus on His power to save." Focus on Christ. That's the answer! I knew that. I'm sure that I had said those same words to others in need. Now I was the one in desperate need. Focus on Christ. It sounds so simple. Focus on Christ. I can do that! Yet, at that very moment, I didn't really know how to do it. I felt very much like the father who pleaded with the Lord to heal his deaf and dumb son, who was possessed by an evil spirit.

And they brought him unto [Jesus]: and when he saw him, straightway the spirit tare him; and he fell on the ground, and wallowed foaming.

And he asked his father, How long is it ago since this came unto him? And he said, Of a child.

And ofttimes it hath cast him into the fire, and into the waters, to destroy him: but if thou canst do any thing, have compassion on us, and help us.

Jesus said unto him, If thou canst believe, all things are possible to him that believeth.

And straightway the father of the child cried out, and said with tears, *Lord, I believe; help thou mine unbelief* (Mark 9:20–24; emphasis added).

I testify that the Lord helps us with our unbelief, with our weaknesses, with our common and uncommon struggles in life, even when we drop to the deepest of our emotional depths. He continues to be close even when we don't recognize it. And, in great blessing to the hundreds of missionaries and others who relied on me and leaned on my strength, He helped me to do my appointed duty (even in my difficulty) in such a way that few others ever realized the challenge I was facing each day. That was one of the Savior's "tender mercies" to me—a gift of grace in the truest sense of the word.

It helps me to know that I have not been alone in such difficulties. Several years ago I was in attendance in an informal gathering of BYU religion faculty as Elder Jeffrey R. Holland shared with us an experience he had shortly after his call to the Quorum of the Twelve Apostles. He spoke of his feelings of absolute inadequacy and how overwhelmed he felt. The candor with which he spoke was both surprising and inspiring. It endeared him to me to know that someone so capable, so talented, so righteous, so faithful could actually feel overwhelmed and inadequate. He mentioned how he had walked the floor at night, searching his soul, "wrestling" with the Lord in his efforts to be cleansed and qualified to serve as a special witness of Christ. "Both my call to the

First Quorum of the Seventy in 1989 and now to the apostleship have involved real soul searching and genuine spiritual examination," Elder Holland later said in an interview for *Brigham Young Magazine.*

But this call, in particular, has caused me deep physical and spiritual anguish. I know, intellectually, what has happened, but from an emotional and spiritual standpoint, accepting the reality is going to take a very long time.

Since this call came, I have gone many nights without sleep. The magnitude of this responsibility has just been consuming (in James P. Bell, "An Apostolic Call," *Brigham Young Magazine,* August 1994, 23).

In the meeting with the religion faculty, Elder Holland poignantly and emotionally explained that during this overwhelming experience he lost all confidence in himself, in his ability to lead, to preach, and to teach. He somewhat jokingly stated that in the condition that he found himself at that time he would not be able to "lead a Primary class out of a brown paper bag."

While I am not trying to compare my breakdown in any way to the buffetings and the sacred, sanctifying influences that Elder Holland and those called to the holy apostleship must undergo, I think there is a lesson to be learned for each of us. I am sure that Elder Holland had great faith, a powerful testimony, loads of talent, and ample ability even before his call to the Twelve. But, as he explained to us, his painful experience impelled him in a new and different way to totally trust in, turn to, and lean on the Savior. His success, strength, and confidence would come not from his own abilities, but from his complete consecration and absolute focus on Christ. I can relate to his experience, and my mind has returned to his words many times. I understand a little better now, because of my own personal experiences, than when Elder Holland spoke to us in 1994.

A General Authority that I spoke with concerning some of our missionary challenges explained to me that the Lord will at times strip away from us our "comfort blankets" and expose our weaknesses and inadequacies so as to "force us to our knees." I am convinced that each of us—if we are faithful and earnestly strive to be true disciples—will be "forced to our knees" at some time in our lives—perhaps many times. For me it was being a mission president. For Elder Holland it was his call as an Apostle. For others it may be a serious health problem, a broken marriage, a prodigal child, the loss of a loved one—any number of life's great traumas. Yet it may not be any one big trauma, but the cumulative effects of the day-to-day battering and bruising that we experience in mortality.

Instead of thinking of these trying moments—whether they be short or long—as crosses to carry or as just more burdens to shoulder, we should see them as evidence of the Lord's grace and "tender mercies" (1 Nephi 1:20). Sister Patricia Holland perhaps stated it best in the previously cited interview conducted shortly after Elder Holland's call to the Twelve. "I think one of the purposes of having this humbling period in our lives," she said, "is so that we will listen and learn" ("An Apostolic Call," 25). Being "forced to our knees" can be an invaluable opportunity to "listen and learn" in new ways.

Now to "the rest of the story" of Jesus and Peter walking on the Sea of Galilee. We often emphasize Peter's "failure" and the Master's rebuke: "O thou of little faith, wherefore didst thou doubt?" (Matthew 14:31). To me, this story is not one of failure or lack of faith, but one of triumph. The focus should not be on Peter's "sinking" but on Christ's "lifting." I am convinced that Peter became far stronger from "sinking" than had he continued to walk on water. If he had walked to the Savior and then back to the boat, no doubt, the other disciples would have been in awe of the miracle. Without being too irreverent, I can imagine that there would have been "high fives" all around and pats on Peter's back.

His triumph, however, came later—in a different way, in what he learned from the Master, and in what he became because of this experience—a transformation that resulted from "sinking" and then allowing the Lord to rescue him.

"And when they were come into the ship, the wind ceased" (Matthew 14:32)—a short and simple verse that raises many questions. How far were Peter and Jesus away from the boat? How did Jesus lift Peter out of the water? How did they get back to the boat? The scriptural record is silent with regard to those things, but perhaps in that silence we can see the message of the miracle. I believe that Jesus caught hold of Peter by the hand and lifted him back to the surface, like a father would lift a child who has fallen back to his feet. To me the miracle is not so much that Peter may have taken a step or two on the surface of the water at first, but rather, that after he cried, "Lord, save me," and caught hold of the Savior's outstretched hand, he walked back to the boat—with the Master.

"Of a truth thou art the Son of God," the disciples cried out in amazement. "What manner of man is this, that even the winds and the sea obey him!" (Matthew 8:27). What manner of man indeed! No wonder the disciples glorified God! Not only did Jesus walk on water and silence storms by His very word, but He enabled Peter to do the same. What a great learning experience for Peter and each of us—when "walking on water" by yourself, you will always sink, but when you focus on Christ, take hold of His outstretched hand of grace, and walk with Him, you cannot fail.

That is what Wendy was tenderly teaching me as she held me in her arms when I was sinking and on the verge of spiritually drowning. She assured me that I would be all right. "Focus on Christ," she repeated. Being focused was a matter of life and death. I couldn't afford to "look beyond the mark" (see Jacob 4:14). I wanted desperately to see clearly the saving hand of grace that would lift me up. I needed all the focus I could muster to take hold of that hand and walk with Him.

In the months and years since that experience, I have learned many things about what it means to focus on Christ and to take hold of His outstretched hand. I probably would never have learned how to do that if I had not been forced to my knees. Just as Peter paid more attention to the words of the Master when he was floundering in the water than when he took his first steps out of the boat, so, too, did I listen and learn more in pain than I ever did in comfort and prosperity. I may never have learned how to focus on Christ if I hadn't been in a position where I absolutely had to do so. Taking hold of His hand and allowing Him to lift us doesn't happen automatically or quickly. It is a spiritual skill that has to be learned and relearned, and then that learning must be continually applied. The chapters that follow will share some of the lessons I have learned about how to do that.

Look unto me in every thought; doubt not, fear not.

—D&C 6:36

2

THINK ON HIM

IT IS EASY TO SAY "FOCUS ON CHRIST," but doing so is a lot more difficult at times. I knew what I needed to do, but in my moment of desperation I didn't know exactly how to do it. Amidst my anxiety attacks and feeling like I was physically, emotionally, and spiritually falling apart at the seams, my wife held me in her arms and talked me through my crisis. The talk therapy she provided, as lifesaving as it was at that moment, was really nothing more than verbally focusing my thoughts. "Visualize the Savior holding you in His arms," Wendy said. "Listen to His words of love." She guided my thoughts to His ministry, recounting some of His miracles and teachings. As she helped me to "focus on Christ," the shaking subsided and the dark emotional clouds of self-doubt and mental anguish lifted a little. The more I thought about the Savior the less I thought about me—my problems, my inadequacies, my homesickness, and a myriad of other self-centered thoughts. It really works!

The human mind is "wired" in such a way that only one thought can be in the mind at a time. Even though we may think that we are mentally "multitasking" a zillion different thoughts, in reality, we can focus on only one thought at a time. The space between thoughts may be smaller than nanoseconds, but each thought occupies its own moment in time. "Did you know that you can only think of one thing at a time?" President Boyd K. Packer taught. "Did you know that every time you think a good thought, there is no room for a bad one? . . . It is important that we know this because then we can give priority to significant and important thoughts" (*That All May Be Edified,*" 35). President Packer then shared an experience that illustrates the importance of giving proper priority to our thoughts.

> When I was about ten years old, we lived in a home surrounded by an orchard. There never seemed to be enough water for the trees. The ditches were always fresh-plowed in the spring, but after the first few irrigating turns, the weeds would spring up in the ditch bottoms and soon they were choked with water grass, June grass, and redroot. One day, in charge of the irrigating turn, I found myself in trouble. As the water moved down the rows choked with weeds, it carried enough leaves and grass and debris to lodge against the weed stocks and flood the water from the ditch. I raced through the puddles, trying to build the banks up a little higher, to the keep the water in the channel. As soon as I had one break patched up there would be another one flooding over in another spot.
>
> About that time an older brother came through the lot with a friend of his who was majoring in agriculture. He watched me for a moment, then with a few vigorous strokes of the shovel he cleared the weeds from the dampened ditch bottom and allowed the water to course through the channel he had dug.
>
> "You will waste the whole irrigating turn patching up the

banks," he said. "If you want the water to stay on its course, you have to make a place for it to go."

I have learned that thoughts, like water, will follow the course if we *make* a place for them to go. Otherwise, we may spend all our time frantically patching up the banks and may find that our "turn" is over and that we have wasted the day of our probation (*"That All May Be Edified,"* 37; emphasis in original).

What Wendy was doing in helping me "focus on Christ" was not just a visualization exercise (like "going to my happy place" when the dentist is drilling my teeth) or mere distraction, but a redirection of thoughts, providing a channel for my thoughts—a replacement of negative, destructive thoughts with ennobling and empowering thoughts.

Don't think that I am oversimplifying or dismissing the seriousness of your problems and predicament. I am not. When I speak about controlling thoughts I am not, in any way whatsoever, saying, "Just snap out of it" or "Don't worry. Be happy." Positive mental attitude has its place, but thinking on Christ is a different thing—a spiritual process that is infinitely higher than the methods or coping mechanisms offered by pop psychology. Even with Wendy encouraging me to visualize spiritual things and to focus on Christ, I didn't immediately jump out of my "bed of affliction." I didn't suddenly become a knight in shining armor, "slay the dragon," marry the princess, and live "happily ever after." (Can you tell that I have been watching a lot of *Sleeping Beauty* and *Cinderella* with grandchildren?)

Although I did marry my princess (in fact, she is a queen), I haven't yet achieved the "happily ever after" part—the fairy-tale life of total joy, no sorrow, no problems, no pain, just perpetual bliss. Certainly, there are plenty of "dragons"—temporal, emotional, and spiritual—that we all have to battle each day. There are discouragements, personal and family problems, bills to pay, mouths to feed, difficulties and drudgeries and unfulfilled expectations—my own and others. That is what life entails. That is what mortals must experience and endure—to live through and learn from. It isn't a fairy tale. It is reality, and reality requires total focus to spiritually survive and thrive in these challenging times.

In the months and years since Wendy had to literally take me by the hand and help me focus on Christ, I have come to a greater appreciation of the many ways God has provided for us to continually turn our thoughts to the Savior. As we better understand, appreciate, and more abundantly avail ourselves of these, the more we will gain vital emotional and spiritual strength. For some like me, who have experienced "crashes" of many sorts, these means of spiritual refocus or rehabilitation get us back on our feet, figuratively (and sometimes literally) speaking. For others (which in reality includes all of us at other times of our lives), they provide a form of spiritual and emotional preventative health care. They are forms of worship—both public and private—whereby we "focus on Christ" and think on Him.

"The Song of the Righteous Is a Prayer unto Me"

One of the most significant ways in which I can "think on Him" is through music. I am no musician. I can't carry a tune in a bucket or a backhoe, but I love music, particularly sacred hymns of praise and the anthems of the Restoration. "Some of the greatest sermons are preached by the singing of hymns," wrote the First Presidency in the preface of our current hymnbook. "Hymns move us to repentance and good works, build testimony and faith, comfort the weary, console the mourning, and inspire us to endure to the end" (*Hymns,* ix). You don't have to sing well or read music to benefit from the hymns. Who wouldn't want to receive blessings such as greater faith and testimony, comfort when weary, consolation when sorrowful, inspiration and motivation when we are "running on empty"? No wonder President Boyd K. Packer has urged us to "choose from among the sacred music of the Church one favorite hymn" and to memorize the words and music and think through that hymn in times of need—whether it be times of temptation, discouragement, sorrow, or loss of direction or desire. He promised that "it will change the whole mood on the stage of your mind" (*That All May Be Edified,* 38–39). Sacred music is one of the most powerful means whereby we can focus on Christ. It is a gift of grace.

Although I have known of President Packer's teachings on controlling thoughts through inspiring music for many years and have taught that concept hundreds of times in formal classroom settings and in private counseling with Church members, I had to relearn it and apply it in my own time of need. Wendy taught it to me both by precept and example. Through the years I have observed her as she has dealt with stress, anxiety, depression (and irritation with me) by either singing a hymn or listening to hymns. It has been so common in our home that I have almost become programmed—when I hear hymns playing on the stereo or hear her singing or humming Church music I suspect that she is struggling a bit. On our mission, when she would get stressed or discouraged, out would come the hymns. On one such occasion, I tenderly asked, "Are you struggling with something? Can I help in some way?" To which she replied, "No, everything is fine. I just love that hymn."

I learned from my own experience that when I hear or sing a hymn I love, everything is fine. I do indeed find greater solace and strength. Yet asking me to name my favorite hymn is like asking me to identify my favorite scripture or select a favorite grandchild. My particular need at a given moment determines my "favorite" hymn. But here is a sampling of some of those hymns that have soothed my soul, quieted my fears, and given courage and inspiration.

Jesus, the very thought of thee
With sweetness fills my breast;
But sweeter far thy face to see
And in thy presence rest.

Nor voice can sing, nor heart can frame,
Nor can the mem'ry find
A sweeter sound than thy blest name,
O Savior of mankind!

O hope of ev'ry contrite heart,
O joy of all the meek,
To those who fall, how kind thou art!
How good to those who seek!

Jesus, our only joy be thou,
As thou our prize wilt be;
Jesus, be thou our glory now,
And thru eternity.

—"Jesus, the Very Thought of Thee," *Hymns,* no. 141

Be still, my soul: The Lord is on thy side;
With patience bear thy cross of grief or pain.
Leave to thy God to order and provide;
In ev'ry change he faithful will remain.
Be still, my soul: Thy best, thy heav'nly Friend
Thru thorny ways leads to a joyful end.

—"Be Still, My Soul," *Hymns,* no. 124

Where can I turn for peace?
Where is my solace
When other sources cease to make me whole? . . .

Who, who can understand?
He, only One.

— "Where Can I Turn for Peace?" *Hymns,* no. 129

Abide with me! fast falls the eventide;
The darkness deepens. Lord, with me abide!
When other helpers fail and comforts flee,
Help of the helpless, oh, abide with me!

Swift to its close out ebbs out life's little day.
Earth's joys grow dim; its glories pass away.
Change and decay in all around I see;
O thou who changest not, abide with me!

I need thy presence ev'ry passing hour.
What but thy grace can foil the tempter's pow'r?
Who, like thyself, my guide and stay can be?
Thru cloud and sunshine, Lord, abide with me!

— "Abide with Me!" *Hymns,* no. 166

I will not doubt, I will not fear;
God's love and strength are always near.
His promised gift helps me to find
An inner strength and peace of mind.
I give the Father willingly
My trust, my prayers, humility.
His Spirit guides; his love assures
That fear departs when faith endures.

— "When Faith Endures," *Hymns,* no. 128

Redeemer of Israel,
Our only delight,

On whom for a blessing we call,
Our shadow by day
And our pillar by night,
Our King, our Deliv'rer, our all! . . .

Restore, my dear Savior,
The light of thy face;
Thy soul-cheering comfort impart;
And let the sweet longing
For thy holy place
Bring hope to my desolate heart.

—"Redeemer of Israel," *Hymns,* no. 6

I know that my Redeemer lives.
What comfort this sweet sentence gives!
He lives, he lives, who once was dead.
He lives, my ever-living Head.
He lives to bless me with his love.
He lives to plead for me above.
He lives my hungry soul to feed.
He lives to bless in times of need.

He lives to grant me rich supply.
He lives to guide me with his eye.
He lives to comfort me when faint.
He lives to hear my soul's complaint.
He lives to silence all my fears.
He lives to wipe away my tears.
He lives to calm my troubled heart.
He lives all blessings to impart.

—"I Know That My Redeemer Lives," *Hymns,* no. 136

I have a small statue in my office of a pioneer family who crossed the plains with a handcart company. Each day I look at it and think of the hymn "Come, Come, Ye Saints." I cannot sing it without thinking of pioneer forebears' sacrifices and dedication. No matter how badly I think I may have it, my problems always pale in comparison. Susanna Stone, a member of the Willie Company, told of the sustaining power of that hymn. "Although we passed through many trying scenes, his protecting care was over us," she later wrote. "I often think of the songs we sang to encourage us on our toilsome journey. It was hard to endure, but the Lord gave us strength and courage. . . . And in the blizzards and falling snow we sat under our handcarts and sang, 'Come, come, ye Saints'" (in Andrew D. Olsen, *The Price We Paid*, 472).

Come, come, ye Saints, no toil nor labor fear;
But with joy wend your way.
Though hard to you this journey may appear,
Grace shall be as your day.
'Tis better far for us to strive
Our useless cares from us to drive;
Do this, and joy your hearts will swell—
All is well! All is well!

Why should we mourn or think our lot is hard?
'Tis not so; all is right.
Why should we think to earn a great reward
If we now shun the fight?
Gird up your loins; fresh courage take.
Our God will never us forsake;
And soon we'll have this tale to tell—
All is well! All is well!

—"Come, Come, Ye Saints," *Hymns*, no. 30

We lived in Israel for a year while I taught at the BYU Jerusalem Center for Near Eastern Studies. One of our favorite field trips included a visit to what we called Micah's Cave (because it was located in the area of the prophet Micah's hometown of Moreshath-Gath). We crawled into the cave on hands and knees. There are some very tight places and some interesting twists and turns to navigate—especially if you are long and tall or what I might delicately refer to as "full-bodied." It is pretty obvious why they call this part of the cave "the birth canal." The cave opens up to a fairly large roomlike chamber. It is so dark you can feel it. It is suffocatingly dark. I would have the students turn off all the flashlights and we would sit silently in the darkness and absorb the feeling of blackness. After a few minutes, which seemed like an eternity if you were claustrophobic, we turned on the flashlights, pulled out our pocket hymnbooks, and sang the hymn "Lead, Kindly Light." It was a powerful teaching moment as we talked about darkness and light—particularly the Light of the world that can chase away all darkness (see D&C 50:25; 88:67). Since then, that hymn has been one of my favorites.

When I was in the depths of depression and anxiety, I felt like I was in an emotional and spiritual Micah's Cave. It was as if I was in a very dark place—with walls moving in on me. It seemed like I was suffocating. My mind returned to those sweet experiences in the Holy Land, and the words of that hymn came to the rescue. Just as the dark was tangible, so too was the light that the hymn gave to my mind and that the Savior gave to my soul. Now as I sing those words they are vivid to me—not just because of my many memorable visits to the "birth canal" cave of Moreshath-Gath, but because of the rescuing light I experienced in one of the darkest periods of my life.

Lead, kindly Light, amid th' encircling gloom;
Lead thou me on!

The night is dark, and I am far from home;
Lead thou me on!
Keep thou my feet; I do not ask to see
The distant scene—one step enough for me.

—"Lead, Kindly Light," *Hymns,* no. 97

I could go on and on. I have so many favorite hymns—so many with special meaning to me or linked closely to some important event or experience in my life. Maybe your favorite hymn isn't one of these I have cited. That's okay. That makes my point exactly. For each of us there are hymns, probably many, that give guidance, hope, and strength. Some rally us to greater courage and motivate us to do more than we may feel we have strength to do. No matter how down I may I feel, I can't stay that way for long when I sing that rousing anthem, "Called to Serve." It always lifts my spirits and brings the best out of me. I have been blessed by that hymn many, many times.

"For my soul delighteth in the song of the heart," the Lord declared, "yea, the song of the righteous is a prayer unto me, and it shall be answered with a *blessing upon their heads*" (D&C 25:12; emphasis added). That promise of a "blessing upon their heads" cannot be overlooked or minimized. Undoubtedly, many blessings are poured out in response to the "song of the righteous," but one of the most significant is what it does to focus our thoughts and our desires on the Savior. No wonder sacred music is such an important part of our Church services. No wonder we sing hymns at funerals, firesides, and even family home evenings (which is somewhat scary when you think of how tone deaf some of us are). It isn't so much a matter of musical ability as it is spiritual feeling. It is a significant way whereby we worship the Lord, think on Him, and learn of Him.

How grateful I am for the power of music in helping me to focus on Christ. How grateful I am that I don't have to wait for Sundays to be blessed by the hymns. I can be blessed by them in my home, in my car, at my office—all the time. Whether or not I have a hymnbook with me, I can sing (especially in the shower where no one else hears me), I can hum or whistle, and I can think of the words and ponder their meaning. I can always have a hymnbook in my head!

"Sweet Hour of Prayer"

"One can pray and yet not really pray," Elder Neal A. Maxwell insightfully observed. "Prayers can be routinized and made very superficial. When this happens, there is very little communication and very little growth. Yet, given the times in which we live, improving our prayers should be one of our deepest desires if we are genuinely serious about growing spiritually" (*All These Things Shall Give Thee Experience*, 91). I know that. I want to have more meaningful prayers. Yet we all, at times, fall into the "routinized" and "superficial" mode of which Elder Maxwell spoke. Thankfully, the Lord periodically provides us with experiences that disrupt the routine and shake us out of superficiality. It is another one of those "tender mercies" that help us to focus on Christ.

Many years ago our two-year-old daughter Janey had a freak accident and fell on her head on our cement driveway. The doctor at the emergency room feared that she had suffered a serious head injury and ordered that she be rushed to a nearby trauma center. Wendy accompanied our baby daughter in the ambulance, and I followed in our car. It was only about fifteen minutes to the trauma center, but it seemed like hours. As I followed the ambulance that carried my injured daughter, I felt totally helpless. All I could do was cry and pray. My prayers during those next several minutes were much different from our family prayer that morning or the blessing on the food at lunch. I was not just "saying prayers." I was truly "crying unto the Lord"—pleading with Him to spare my daughter. My prayer at that moment was not just something on my list of things to do each day, but rather a matter of life and death. Fortunately, my heartfelt pleas that day were mercifully answered and Janey fully recovered.

In a different way, as I struggled with my emotional breakdown while serving as a mission president, prayer became again a matter of life and death—spiritual and emotional life. I have always "said my prayers." Wendy has almost always seen to it that we never leave the house without having family prayer. Presiding over a mission, we prayed more frequently and fervently than perhaps at any other period of time in our lives. Yet when I was forced to my knees in time of extreme need, prayer took on a whole new meaning—maybe not intellectually, for I always knew the concept, but experientially.

The scriptures, particularly the Book of Mormon, speak of prayer as "crying unto the Lord" (see, for example, 1 Nephi 2:16; 17:7; 2 Nephi 33:13; Mosiah 11:24–25; Alma 33:3–11). I don't know about you, but I often think of "crying" in somewhat negative terms. It conjures up images of pain, pleading, sorrowing, and struggling. No doubt "crying unto the Lord" involves a great deal of intensity. I experienced that many times on our mission. I was a frequent "guest" in the master bedroom closet of the mission home. There was indeed pain, suffering, and soulful petitions. But there was something more—something that I am not sure I would have become as familiar with had I not been so overcome by feelings of inadequacy, fear, and self-doubt and had I not had to confront a mountain of problems and pressures head-on. I found prayer to be a dear friend, not just a spiritual life preserver or safety net. Just as hymns help us to focus on Christ, so can prayer. It can and should be a time of spiritual rejuvenation, a time of sweetness, not just a time to rattle off a long list of needs—however great those needs may be. Prayer allows me to clear my mind of lesser matters and focus on the things of God. What a supernal blessing it is to be able to quiet our minds and surroundings, approach our God in prayer, and think on Him.

> Sweet hour of prayer! Sweet hour of prayer!
> That calls me from a world of care
> And bids me at my Father's throne
> Make all my wants and wishes known.
> In seasons of distress and grief,
> My soul has often found relief
> And oft escaped the tempter's snare
> By thy return, sweet hour of prayer!
>
> Sweet hour of prayer! Sweet hour of prayer!
> Thy wings shall my petition bear
> To him whose truth and faithfulness
> Engage the waiting soul to bless.
> And since he bids me seek his face,
> Believe his word, and trust his grace,
> I'll cast on him my ev'ry care,
> And wait for thee, sweet hour of prayer!
>
> —"Sweet Hour of Prayer," *Hymns,* no. 142

The great Book of Mormon prophet Amulek taught that we can pray any time, in any place, and about any matter. "Cry unto him for mercy; for he is mighty to save" (Alma 34:18). "Cry unto him in your houses, yea, over all your household, both morning, mid-day, and evening" (Alma 34:21). He counseled us to pray about our temporal concerns and our emotional and spiritual needs. "Pour out your souls in your closets, and your secret places, and in your wilderness" (Alma 34:26). Most significantly, Amulek reminds us that when we are not on our knees in prayer, "let your hearts be full, drawn out in prayer unto him continually for your welfare, and also for the welfare of those who are around you" (Alma 34:27).

I began to understand in a more profound way what Amulek meant by this and perhaps what Enos experienced in his wrestle with God in mighty prayer that spanned all the day long and into the night (see Enos 1:2–4). I don't think Enos was on his knees all that time and I am not sure that he prayed vocally for many, many hours. I am sure, however, that his mind, heart, and soul were "drawn out in prayer unto [God] continually." His communion with God included vocal petitions and mental pondering. His "mighty prayer" probably involved being on his knees for a long, long time, but also getting up off his knees, sitting and pondering, walking and talking with the Lord hour upon hour. As I struggled with my role as mission president and my own emotional frailties, I, like Enos, wrestled with God in mighty prayer. That wrestle was not just when I was on my knees. It was a process of continual communion.

Sometimes, as strange as it may sound, my most "sweet hour of prayer" as I struggled so mightily came not in the closet, beside my bed, or by my desk in the mission office, but when I was driving in the car or taking a walk. This was a way whereby I could collect my thoughts, focus on Christ, think on Him, and talk with God. I didn't close my eyes, bow my head, and fold my arms (none of which are recommended when driving), but I did communicate with mouth, mind, heart, and soul. Those times are indeed "sweet." How thankful I am that I can focus on Christ in prayer any time, any place. Whether it be on a walk observing the beauties of nature, driving in the car, working in the garden, or sitting in a boring meeting staring at the walls, I can have a full heart—"drawn out in prayer . . . continually."

Doctors and therapists often say that physical exercise is the most helpful prescription for those suffering from depression and anxiety. I am convinced that the spiritual benefits can be as great as, if not greater than, the physical benefits, if we use that time of refreshment to think on Him and talk to Him. If I will allow my mind, heart, and soul to be drawn out continually in prayer I am never alone. I know that to be true.

"This Do in Remembrance of Me"

One of the most significant and sacred ways in which we can turn our thoughts to the Savior and commune with Deity is through the sacrament of the Lord's Supper. I found, as I was emotionally struggling so mightily, that partaking of the sacrament was a source of great spiritual strength and that those quiet, reverent moments during its administration served as a spiritual oasis—"a refuge from the storm" (D&C 115:6). Not only do we renew our covenants with the worthy partaking of the emblems of the Lord's supreme sacrifice, but we also receive anew the promise of having the Holy Ghost as our constant companion, our sanctifier, our guide and comforter. It is this ordinance that makes sacrament meeting "the *most sacred,* the *most holy,* of all the meetings of the Church" (Joseph Fielding Smith, *Doctrines of Salvation,* 2:340; emphasis in original). The Savior commanded His disciples, both ancient and modern, to regularly participate in this holy, saving ordinance that is "in the remembrance of the Lord Jesus" (D&C 20:75; see also Moroni 4–5; 3 Nephi 18:5–12; Luke 22:17–20).

In His grace, God has granted to us an opportunity each week to focus on Christ—not only by covenanting that we will "always remember him" (D&C 20:77, 79), but also by remembering Christ and thinking on Him for those few minutes. I wonder if we realize how important, how powerful, how sustaining those moments really are. I know that (although I may be suffering from a bad case of the "Sunday dreads" because of speaking assignments, leadership responsibilities, or, in days past, the anticipation of wrestling children during sacrament meeting) those moments during the administration of the sacrament become sacred space that brings me back to and focuses my mind on what and who matter most. Elder Jeffrey R. Holland has given some suggestions on what we can remember and think about as we focus on Christ during the sacrament:

> We could remember the Savior's premortal life and all that we know Him to have done as the great Jehovah, creator of heaven and earth and all things that in them are. We could remember that even in the grand council of heaven He loved us and was wonderfully strong, that we triumphed even there by the power of Christ and our faith in the blood of the Lamb (see Rev. 12:10 11). . . .
>
> We could remember Christ's miracles and His teachings, His healings and His help. We could remember that He gave sight to the blind and hearing to the deaf and motion to the lame and the maimed and the withered. Then, on those days when we feel our progress has halted or our joys and views have grown dim, we can press forward steadfastly in Christ, with unshaken faith in Him and a perfect brightness of hope (see 2 Ne. 31:19–20).
>
> We could remember that even with such a solemn mission given to Him, the Savior found delight in living; He enjoyed people and told His disciples to be of good cheer. He said we should be as thrilled with the gospel as one who had found a great treasure, a veritable pearl of great price, right on our own doorstep. We could remember that Jesus found special joy and happiness in children and said all of us should be more like them—guileless and pure, quick to laugh and to love and to forgive, slow to remember any offense. . . .
>
> We could—and should—remember the wonderful things that have come to us in our lives and that "all things which are

good cometh of Christ" (Moro. 7:24). Those of us who are so
blessed could remember the courage of those around us who
face more difficulty than we, but who remain cheerful, who do
the best they can, and trust that the Bright and Morning Star
will rise again for them—as surely He will do (see Rev. 22:16).

On some days we will have cause to remember the unkind
treatment He received, the rejection He experienced, and the
injustice—oh, the injustice—He endured. When we, too, then
face some of that in life, we can remember that Christ was also
"troubled on every side, [but] not distressed; . . . perplexed, but
not in despair; persecuted, but not forsaken; cast down, but not
destroyed" (2 Cor. 4:8–9).

When those difficult times come to us, we can remember
that Jesus had to descend below all things before He could
ascend above them, and that He suffered pains and afflictions
and temptations of every kind that He might be filled with
mercy and know how to succor His people in their infirmities
(see Alma 7:11–12; D&C 88:6).

All this we could remember when we are invited by a
kneeling young priest to remember Christ always (*Trusting
Jesus,* 21–24).

How grateful I am that I have this sacred privilege each week to sing
hymns of worship, to hear the sacramental prayers and add my "Amen,"
to partake of the emblems of the Savior's broken body and spilled blood
in my behalf, and to reverently think on Him. What a blessing to have
this opportunity to focus on Christ and feel Him close.

"Let Virtue Garnish Thy Thoughts Unceasingly"

During my three years as mission president there weren't very many
days (if any) when I didn't have to give "pep talks" to discouraged

missionaries or counsel an elder or sister who was struggling with unworthy thoughts and desires. Countless times I have used President Boyd K. Packer's counsel concerning controlling thoughts by singing hymns and thinking about the Savior—about how we can chase bad thoughts off the stage of our mind with good thoughts, noble thoughts, worthy thoughts. On one occasion, as I counseled an elder I received a revelation—an unexpected, but much-needed, revelation. The elder confided in me his struggle with feelings of worthlessness because of past sins. It was not a matter of unworthiness, for he had fully repented and was temple-worthy. In fact, he was one of the finest missionaries we had in our mission. He was a giant of a leader among his peers, and the people loved and respected him. He explained to me that he felt that when he needed the Spirit the most in his ministry, he would be beset with memories of these past sins. In turn, he would feel unworthy and wonder if he had adequately repented. Other self-defeating and self-demeaning thoughts would creep onto the stage of his mind.

"Don't go there!" I told him. "You just can't allow your mind to entertain such thoughts." I told him that Satan wanted him to beat himself up because that would weaken his faith and prevent him from doing and being what the Lord desired of him. I then shared with him an analogy I had heard Elder Richard G. Scott share in general conference many years earlier.

If you, through poor judgment, were to cover your shoes with mud, would you leave them that way? Of course not. You would cleanse and restore them. Would you then gather the residue of mud and place it in an envelope to show others the mistake that you made? No. Neither should you continue to relive forgiven sin. Every time such thoughts come into your mind, turn your heart in gratitude to the Savior, who gave His life that we, through faith in Him and obedience to His teachings, can overcome transgression and conquer its depressing influence in our lives ("We Love You—Please Come Back," *Ensign,* May 1986, 12).

I tried my best to explain to the young elder that when we have experienced the cleansing power of the Atonement in our lives we have to close the door on the past mistakes and never open that door again. I urged him with all the energy of my soul to slam the door shut on such self-punishing thoughts. I paraphrased what I remembered from Elder Scott's inspired talk. "Satan would encourage you to continue to relive the details of past mistakes, knowing that such thoughts make progress, growth, and service difficult to attain. It is as though Satan ties strings to the mind and body so that he can manipulate one like a puppet, discouraging personal achievement" ("We Love You—Please Come Back," 11). As I was waxing eloquent, the revelation came: I needed this counsel more than the elder did. It hit me like a ton of bricks. I was the sick physician trying to heal others—a hypocritical doctor who wouldn't take the medicine he prescribed.

My situation was different, but the principle was the same. By focusing so much on my feelings of inadequacy and the problems and pressures I faced, I actually was doing the same thing. My thoughts were keeping me in emotional and spiritual bondage. They were not lustful thoughts, but they were unworthy just the same—unworthy because they prevented me from focusing on Christ, rising up, and being a man of God. "Don't go there!" my own words echoed in my ears. "You just can't allow your mind to entertain such thoughts."

Did I really believe what I so passionately had taught the missionaries in general and this elder in particular? In that moment I realized, in a way never before experienced, that controlling my thoughts was what the Lord expected of me. It is an essential act of faith in Christ.

Dismissing thoughts of self-contempt, self-pity, and self-doubt is just as vital as dismissing immoral thoughts from the stage of my mind.

"Let virtue garnish thy thoughts *unceasingly,*" the Lord admonished in our day (D&C 121:45; emphasis added). Virtue doesn't merely refer to being clean. It also refers to power—the power of God. We are all familiar with the story of Jesus' healing of the woman with the "issue of blood" (see Matthew 9:20–22; Luke 8:43–48). There is an interesting phrase in Luke's account that has taken on new meaning to me. When the woman touched the hem of the Master's cloak, He said, "I perceive that virtue is gone out of me." Clearly, the word *virtue* in that context did not mean moral purity—that never left Jesus. The Greek word for virtue in this passage is *arate,* which means power and strength. The Prophet Joseph Smith elaborated: "The virtue here referred to is *the spirit of life*" (*Teachings of the Prophet Joseph Smith,* 281; emphasis added).

Do you see that virtue is power—Christlike power, godly power, life-giving and life-strengthening power. So when the Lord commands us to "let virtue garnish thy thoughts unceasingly," He is commanding us not only to chase out of our minds immoral and impure thoughts, but also to eliminate those thoughts that would sap our spiritual strength and leave us powerless. In essence we are commanded: Let the power that comes from focusing on Christ garnish thy thoughts unceasingly. And for all other thoughts and feelings that push down instead of lift up, that focus on self instead of focusing on Christ, the answer is— "Don't go there! You just can't allow your mind to entertain such thoughts."

That was my revelation. That was what the Lord wanted me to learn, not just talk about. I still have my moments of weakness, worry, and self-doubt when I have to give myself that same "pep talk" about controlling my thoughts. It is a continual struggle—a struggle that is made easier by utilizing those gifts of grace that help me to think on Him.

> *May Christ lift thee up, and may his sufferings and death, and the showing his body unto our fathers, and his mercy and long-suffering, and the hope of his glory and of eternal life, rest in your mind forever.*

—Moroni 9:25

3

THANK HIM

NOT MANY MONTHS BEFORE MY father passed away, I had the privilege of learning from him one of the most important lessons of my life—a lesson that would help me through some difficult and trying times of my own. My mother had died unexpectedly about a year earlier. Quite understandably, it was difficult for Dad to be alone. He and Mom had been married for sixty-one years. I worried about how he would fare on his own. I had never seen my father's homemaking skills in action. I don't think he even knew how to boil water, and I know he didn't care for cold cereal. He hadn't been exposed to ramen noodles or boxed macaroni and cheese like our busy family, so I was concerned about whether he would have enough to eat. (Little did I know at the time, but several of the "widow ladies"—as my father referred to them—in Dad's stake graciously brought him casseroles, soups, salads, and all kinds of desserts. Not only was he not starving, he had become a hot commodity in senior-citizen social circles!) There were many things I was concerned about and discussed with him. How was his health? Did he need any help with the house? Was there enough money to pay the bills? What could I do to help him? He must have felt like I was conducting some sort of interrogation as I peppered him with all of these questions. I guess I was.

Dad had wanted me to drive him to some of the places of his childhood and early marriage years. As we drove we talked and reminisced. Trying to be the dutiful son and feeling a sense of responsibility to care for him in his advanced years, I continued to probe concerning how he was really doing. "Do you have enough money for all of your needs?" I repeatedly asked him. His response didn't fully answer my question. In hindsight, however, I see that he was trying to teach me that there is more to life—an abundant life—than money. He proceeded to list his contributions to the Church and to charity. "You are paying way too much fast offering," I scolded. "You don't have to pay tithing on that income. You have already paid your tithing on that!" After each of his statements about his giving, I added some comment about being careful with his money. "The Lord doesn't expect you to contribute so much," I said, "that you don't have means to care for yourself or to be able to face unexpected needs in the future." I thought it sounded so good— sounded like I was looking out for him and that I was teaching him something profound. I was humbled by his words—words that both rebuked and instructed me.

"I know I don't have to do all this," Dad stated, "but I want to." With quivering lips, tears rolling down his cheeks, and a voice cracking with emotion, he continued, "I want to do this. I can afford it. It is the least I can do, because God has been so good to me."

The concerns I had previously expressed to my dad in my attempt to "protect" him seemed awfully shallow and unimportant at that moment. "Because God has been so good to me." What a simple, yet profound declaration. There was nothing more that needed to be said. In silence, we drove for several minutes with tears streaming down our faces. His words echoed in my ears and pierced my soul. "Because God has been so good to me." When we could finally speak, we spoke of

God's goodness—His goodness to each of us, to our families, to our friends and loved ones, to our nation.

"Because God has been so good to me" wasn't just something that my father said at that moment to shut me up. It wasn't just a nice sentiment that would look great in a greeting card. "Because God has been so good to me" was how he lived his life. As I looked at my father, I saw an elderly man with wrinkles and white hair (most of which I probably caused). I saw a man who had faced his share of problems and pressures, a man who had known loss and disappointment. I saw a man who certainly carried his share of grief and loneliness. I saw a man who, though he didn't say much about it, must have been in considerable pain and discomfort as cancer, unbeknownst to any of us, was at that moment ravaging his body. Yet despite all this and more, his focus was not on himself or his woes but on his blessings. I was so proud of him. I was inspired by him. I wanted to be like him. "Because God has been so good to me" was how I wanted to live my life.

At the moment my father said those immortal words I was inspired, but I could not have known what a power they would become in my life. A few years later they would become a very real lifeline. When I was in the dark hole of depression and feeling so overwhelmed with life, I learned that one of the most important ways to focus on Christ is to focus on the multitude of tender mercies He extends to us in our lives. It takes real effort to "count your many blessings" when the natural man wants to wallow in self-pity and focus on pain and problems. Have you ever noticed how difficult it is to look at life as a glass half full instead of as a glass half empty when we are discouraged and depressed, beset by hardships and heartaches? It takes effort—spiritual and emotional effort. When we are down in the dumps it is easy to drown our sorrows with cupcakes and ice cream (or whatever your favorite comfort food may be), but it takes real effort to go to the gym and have a strenuous workout.

Why is that? I think the answer is that the natural man always seeks the path of least resistance—both physically and spiritually. That is why it takes real effort to focus on Christ. While it may be easy (and almost always a waste of time and energy) to dwell on all of our problems, it takes conscious effort to think about the many ways God has blessed us. It takes faith to think about, really believe, and then live in a way that bespeaks "because God has been so good to me."

I know what I'm talking about. I've been there. I've spent plenty of wallowing time in life's "pity potholes." It is easy to do. Unfortunately, those pity potholes are nothing more than emotional quicksand. If you don't stop flailing away, you'll surely sink and drown. Our only hope in that condition—in all the conditions and circumstances of our lives—is to reach out and grab on to the rescuing arm of "him who is mighty to save" (2 Nephi 31:19).

I had to learn that the hard way. I have had a mouthful of sand and water, figuratively speaking. I have experienced more emotional quicksand than I needed to, because it took me so long to focus on Him and take hold of His rescuing hand.

One of the most important lessons I have learned through experience is that gratitude is an antidote to selfishness—counting blessings puts problems and pains in perspective. We frequently sing the hymn "Count Your Blessings." As we sing, do we ponder the meaning of the words? Do we really believe them? Do we trust in the promises?

> When upon life's billows you are tempest-tossed,
> When you are discouraged, thinking all is lost,
> Count your many blessings; name them one by one,
> And it will surprise you what the Lord has done.
>
> Are you ever burdened with a load of care?
> Does the cross seem heavy you are called to bear?
> Count your many blessings; ev'ry doubt will fly,
> And you will be singing as the days go by.

When you look at others with their lands and gold,
Think that Christ has promised you his wealth untold.
Count your many blessings; money cannot buy
Your reward in heaven nor your home on high.

So amid the conflict, whether great or small,
Do not be discouraged; God is over all.
Count your many blessings; angels will attend,
Help and comfort give you to your journey's end.

—"Count Your Blessings," *Hymns*, no. 241

Gratitude: An Expression of Faith and a Saving Principle

When I served as a bishop many years ago, I would come home emotionally drained after a Sunday or weeknight full of interviews, hearing confessions of serious sins, and listening to and counseling ward members about their problems. It was a heavy burden at times. Sometimes I didn't know what to say or do to help, but always I came home grateful for my own problems. That is one of the great blessings of service in the Church—we realize that there is always someone who has greater problems and carries heavier burdens than we do. However, the gratitude I felt then was not so much counting blessings as an attitude of "Boy, I'm glad I'm not them." It was passive—appreciation by default—rather than actively, consciously, purposefully acknowledging and expressing deep gratitude for the Lord's blessings in my life.

"Thank the Lord thy God in all things," the Lord has declared in our day. "And in nothing doth man offend God, or against none is his wrath kindled, save those who confess not his hand in all things, and obey not his commandments" (D&C 59:7, 21). An unwillingness to acknowledge God's goodness and express profound gratitude for His blessings in our lives not only offends God, but it offends the Spirit and diminishes its strengthening and comforting influence in our lives. No wonder President James E. Faust spoke of gratitude as "more than a social courtesy; it is a binding commandment." Giving heartfelt thanks to the Lord for His tender mercies is, as President Faust taught, "an expression of faith and . . . a saving principle" ("Gratitude As a Saving Principle," *Ensign,* May 1990, 85). It is a saving principle because it saves us from self-absorption and shortsightedness. It saves us from feeling abandoned or that no one cares. Gratitude saves us from wasting our spiritual and emotional powers when we focus so much on how bad we have it, what we don't have, or how we wish things were different.

On our first Thanksgiving Day in the mission field I was feeling pretty sorry for myself. Still struggling with depression and anxiety, compounded by the pressures and problems of presiding over a mission, I didn't really feel much like having company for Thanksgiving dinner. I was feeling very homesick—thinking how much better life would be if we were home with our family. I was way down deep in my pity pothole and enjoying the scenery there. I didn't want to be around others because I would have to pretend to be charming and happy.

Yet Wendy knew what I needed, and she wasn't about to let me continue in my self-induced misery. So she invited to the mission home for dinner the elders who were serving as my assistants and the two senior couples who were serving in the mission office. They did not have any idea how miserable I was or the emotional struggles that I was having. Since they didn't know, they didn't really have any reason to try to cheer me up or pull me out of my pothole. They weren't consciously trying to counsel or teach me, but something happened that day that did teach me an important lesson. It was a moment—a simple act, a small gesture—that served as a valuable catalyst for change. Perhaps none of the missionaries that dined with us on that Thanksgiving Day will even remember the moment; to them it was probably no big deal, but to me it was like the dense, dark clouds were giving way (at least a little) to the welcome, warm rays of sunshine.

Just as we were ready to dive in to a sumptuous feast, one of the elders asked, "President, can we do something before we eat?" What was I to say? "No! Be quiet. Let's eat!"? I may have felt that way, but I couldn't say it. The young elder proceeded to tell us that it was a tradition in his family that before they ate their Thanksgiving meal each member of the family would mention some of the things for which they were most thankful. Most of us stated that we had similar traditions in our homes.

For the next several minutes we went around the table counting our blessings. I must admit that I wasn't in the mood for this exercise, and I viewed it as more than a little cheesy. It didn't take long, however, for my bad attitude to melt away. As each missionary around the table expressed heartfelt gratitude for specific blessings—some blessings cited were simple things that are often taken for granted—I began to feel again. I felt a reawakening of gratitude. Almost like a flood, emotions of thanksgiving, joy, and love poured over me. Instead of dwelling totally on my problems, worries, inadequacies, and weaknesses, as I had for the previous months, the veil parted slightly and I could see what a privilege it was to serve with these great people, how blessed my life had been, how much the Lord had done for me. As my gratitude increased, so did my faith in and love for the Lord. Again I heard my father's words: "because God has been so good to me."

"Live in Thanksgiving Daily"

Ingratitude is like a mirror that constantly reflects back to us our problems, weaknesses, and worries. In fact, ingratitude is like those mirrors found in amusement parks and carnivals that distort reality. Failure to see the hand of God in our lives in true perspective actually leaves us with a warped view of our real circumstances and true selves.

On the other hand, gratitude is like a large picture window that allows us a panoramic view of the landscape of God's goodness to us. Gratitude increases our faith in the Lord Jesus Christ, because we recognize His tender mercies in our lives. A thankful heart increases our spiritual strength—strength to endure hardships and heartaches, strength to resist temptation, strength to face difficult tasks and seemingly overwhelming responsibilities. The more we acknowledge and appreciate God's goodness to us, the more we will seek to please Him and trust in Him. With these promised blessings at hand, I want to make every day a Thanksgiving Day. "Live in thanksgiving daily," the Book of Mormon prophet Amulek admonished, "for the many mercies and blessings which he doth bestow upon you" (Alma 34:38).

While on a walk one day, Wendy and I began to talk about the many times we have seen the hand of the Lord in our lives. It may have started out as just casual conversation, but it soon became a deep discussion and a profound spiritual experience. We sat on a park bench and took turns "counting" our blessings—miracles that had been witnessed, prayers that had been answered, and doors that had been opened. The obvious things were easily and quickly identified. The small things— things we took for granted and didn't really think that much about— were seen for the miracles that they are in their own right. "Out of small things proceedeth that which is great" (D&C 64:33). We realized that God had gone before us, as He had for the Israelites as a cloud by day and pillar of fire by night. We couldn't see Him physically, but we could feel His presence and see what He had done.

Awesome is a word that has lost its true significance in this day and age, but it really fits in describing the works of God—big and small—in our lives. We profoundly experienced what the familiar hymn declares: "Count your many blessings; name them one by one, and it will surprise you what the Lord has done" (*Hymns,* no. 241). We were, indeed, surprised. But more than that, we were in awe.

The more I realized what the Lord had done for me, the more I felt guilty for feeling so sorry for myself. It's pretty hard, if not impossible, to say "Woe is me" at the same time you are saying, "How blessed I am." It's pretty hard to say "I can't do this" when you recognize all the ways the Lord has carried you in the past and helped you get through worse things. When I started to really believe this, things changed—not only for me personally, but also for our missionaries. The more grateful I was, the less discouragement and depression I experienced. It worked the same for the elders and sisters in our mission. I came to understand that gratitude doesn't just automatically happen. We cannot "live with thanksgiving daily" without conscientious and consistent effort on our part. While there are undoubtedly many things we can do to foster a spirit of gratitude, there are a couple of things that have helped me to more effectively focus on Christ in greater gratitude.

A "Count Your Blessings" Journal

From the time of President Spencer W. Kimball, we have heard much about the importance of recording the important events and spiritual experiences of our lives in a personal journal. *Preach My Gospel* instructs missionaries (and I certainly emphasized it a great deal as a mission president) to have a study journal to include insights gleaned from personal and companionship scripture study. I have heard Elder Richard G. Scott of the Quorum of the Twelve Apostles counsel that we keep a journal of the promptings of the Holy Ghost in our lives. Each of these different types of journals serves an important spiritual purpose. I began to realize that a "Count Your Blessings" journal could likewise yield spiritual returns. Elder Scott shared a touching example from the journal of his beloved wife, recorded as she was struggling with terminal cancer. It is a great example of a "Count Your Blessings" entry.

"It is a beautiful fall day," Jeanene wrote. "I picked up the mail and sat down on the swing. I was so happy and content in the warm sun, the sweet smell of nature and the trees around me. I just sat and gloried in the fact that I am still alive on this beautiful earth. . . . The Lord is so good to me. How I thank Him that I am still here and feeling so good. I am soooooo happy I just want to shout and dance through this beautiful house as the sun streams into the big windows. I love being alive" (in *Finding Peace, Happiness, and Joy,* 165).

Sister Scott certainly could have complained about her condition, but, instead, recording her gratitude for life's simple joys strengthened her and those around her. Hers is an inspiring example of counting and recording blessings.

I came to the realization of the value of a "Count Your Blessings" journal not only from others' examples, like Sister Scott's, but also through my own experiences and the experiences of our missionaries. In my regular interviews with the missionaries I often heard complaints about everything—the difficulty of the work, constant rejection, "weird" companions, no dinner appointments, too many dinner appointments, homesickness, "Dear Johns," weather that is too hot, weather that is too cold. . . . The list could go on and on and on. I must admit that the more I heard the missionaries complain, the worse I felt about the complaints that I had so vociferously registered with God when I was down in the dumps.

It was in one of those gripe sessions that I had another revelation. As a missionary was going through his long list of complaints and his graphic description about how bad he had it, I gave him an assignment. At the end of each day, he was to write down the good things that he experienced that day. I asked him to look for miracles each day and write down everything and anything that evidenced God's love for him.

As he worked on this assignment, his outlook on life improved dramatically and he became a more effective and powerful missionary. Other elders and sisters who had also received from me this assignment experienced similar results. In fact, I saw a mighty change in the mission. Where before I dreaded to answer my phone because of the problems and complaints that I would hear, now I was excited to hear the missionaries' daily expressions of gratitude for the miracles and blessings they were experiencing. Like my missionaries, as my attitude and gratitude improved, my faith increased. Daily acknowledgment of God's goodness was a simple task that resulted in significant changes.

Recording our feelings of gratitude for the Lord's tender mercies doesn't need to be difficult, complex, or sophisticated. It doesn't have to be in a leather-bound journal. It can be on an index card or a scrap of paper. We can count our blessings in writing at night right before we go to sleep, or we can jot something down whenever we glimpse the goodness of God. I have found it particularly helpful to turn to my "Count Your Blessings" journal when I feel discouraged or inadequate. Recording blessings and reviewing them periodically encourages and inspires. Yet it doesn't matter so much when or how you do it. What matters is that you recognize and record. I promise you that as you do, you will see more, feel more, and become more.

A Prayer of Thanksgiving

Several years ago, in one of my classes, I had a funny experience that also taught a valuable principle. The midterm exam was scheduled to be given that day in class. The student who was called on to offer the opening prayer thought that if he prayed long enough—like the entire class period—they would not have to take the test. The longer he prayed the more upset I became. I thought it was irreverent, and I was about to stop him when the thought entered my mind, "Don't stop him. It will be good for him!"

It wasn't long until he ran out of things to say in his prayer. He had already "blessed" most everything and everyone he could think of. In an effort to keep the prayer going, this young man began again the "We thank thee" portion of the prayer. He had already said the usual, "We thank thee for all of our blessings." When he had to be specific, however, it was harder. Even though I was annoyed, I was still impressed that he remembered so many things for which he was grateful.

I am quite sure that he had never offered such a prayer before, and I am positive that none of us had heard such a prayer. After several minutes (which must have seemed like an hour to him and to the entire class), the prayer ended. The class still had to take the test, but now with significantly less time to complete it. I think we all learned, however, that it is harder than you think to say a long prayer comprised mostly of expressions of thanks. Personally, I wondered what would I say and how long could I actually pray if I didn't ask for blessings but only expressed gratitude. Would my prayer last longer than an obligatory two-and-a-half minutes?

"Gratitude is of the very essence of worship," President Gordon B. Hinckley taught (*Teachings of Gordon B. Hinckley,* 250). Our beloved prophet not only instructed, but he also exemplified this very principle. "When President Gordon B. Hinckley prays in our meetings," Elder Richard G. Scott reported, "more than two-thirds of the content is a sincere expression of gratitude for specific blessings the Lord has granted. Expressing gratitude for as many blessings as one can identify—whether for the Lord or others' thoughtful kindnesses—has multiple compensations" (*Finding Peace, Happiness, and Joy,* 201).

What an inspiring statement! Think of it. Despite all the concerns, difficult issues, complex problems, and overwhelming responsibilities that come with leading a fast-growing, worldwide Church, the prophet's prayers were mostly expressions of gratitude for specific blessings. As Elder Scott observed, expressing gratitude "for as many blessings as one can identify" brings great blessings. Because "gratitude is the very essence of worship," it brings the Spirit into our lives in greater abundance. Greater gratitude yields greater guidance.

Each of us has many needs. We have personal and family responsibilities for which we need guidance. There are problems to address and challenges to face. There are sins to repent of and temptations to resist. We all need God's blessings in our lives. Yet despite all of the myriad of reasons we can petition our Father in Heaven in prayer, we would be well served to periodically pray a prayer of thanksgiving—no requests, no petitions, no pleadings, just heartfelt expressions of gratitude. It is not so much that God needs to hear it (even though I am sure He is pleased) as it is that I need to say it. I am blessed and refocused when I do so. I can sense a difference in myself when I give thanks for simple things—things that I don't often remember to thank Him for, such as indoor plumbing, hot water for my shower, good food to eat, clothes to wear, clean water to drink, a comfortable home, good friends, ears to hear good music and the laughter of my grandchildren, eyes to both read good books and see majestic mountains.

When I have counted my blessings in writing and offered prayers exclusively for the purpose of giving thanks, I have quickly discovered that I have far more reason to say "I thank thee" than "I ask thee." It is a humbling realization, but a strengthening one. A recognition that we are all "unprofitable servants" (see Mosiah 2:21) because of God's goodness, as humbling as it is, actually enriches our relationship with Deity, forges greater faith, and spiritually empowers us. "The grateful man sees so much in the world to be thankful for," President Joseph F. Smith declared, "and with him the good outweighs the evil. Love overpowers jealousy, and light drives darkness out of his life" (*Gospel Doctrine,* 263).

Rich in Blessings

Like all children, our kids had no concept of wealth or poverty when they were very young. It was always interesting to observe how their perceptions of "haves" and "have nots" evolved with time and experience. They did not really understand (nor did they much care about) words such as *rich* or *poor*. They had friends who lived in affluence and others who came from very humble circumstances. They didn't care so much about what their friends' houses were like as much as how kind the other kids were to them or how much fun they had together.

Unfortunately, it didn't remain so innocent and simple. As their horizons broadened, they began to learn of and notice the differences. I remember that when one of our children first learned in school about someone being rich, she came home and matter-of-factly asked, "Are we rich?" I was stunned. I thought the answer to that question was obvious. "No, we are not rich!" I thought, but didn't say. Since I was a teacher with a very modest income, we had always lived on a shoestring budget. I couldn't understand how my daughter could even wonder if we were rich. I took pride in my poverty!

Before I could say anything, Wendy wisely responded, "We are rich in blessings!" That satisfied our daughter—at least for a time. When she became a teenager and faced the harsh reality of what her parents could afford (or mostly not afford), that phrase wasn't as satisfactory.

Through the years, we have used that phrase, "We are in rich blessings," many times and in many ways. Sometimes it meant "We can't afford that, but we are still rich in blessings." Sometimes we would say it in a humorous way when everything seemed to be going wrong—when we felt more like crying than laughing. "Well, at least we are rich in blessings" would always make us feel better and help keep things in proper perspective. "We are rich in blessings" has now become a Top family maxim because the older we get the truer it is. It has always been a true statement, but now we realize more than ever how truly rich we are in blessings. No longer is that statement used merely to placate a child or to make ourselves feel a little better about not having something we really want. It is a true statement—in fact, an understatement. We are rich beyond expression—not in money or property or jewels or fancy cars, but in bounteous blessings received from the Bestower of "the unsearchable riches of Christ" (Ephesians 3:8).

There was a moment while serving our mission that this realization finally began to sink into my hard head and hard heart. The revelation came in a sealing room in the Nauvoo Illinois Temple. Our youngest daughter had just been married for time and all eternity to a wonderful, worthy young man. All of our children were there to witness the joyous occasion. In addition, I felt the presence of loved ones from the other side of the veil. Truly, it was a "heaven on earth" moment. After all of the guests had left the sealing room, I was able to hold Jancy in my arms and express my love. I told her how proud we were of her and how fervently we had prayed for that very moment. "I am here in the temple," she said, "because you and Mom were worthy and willing to serve a mission."

My gratitude was inexpressible. At that moment, I saw things with new eyes. I saw things, including my own challenges, problems, and limitations, with an eternal perspective. That view changed everything. I realized at that moment that whatever difficulty I had to endure, whatever burden I had to bear, whatever problem I had to solve, it was all worth it. I would have paid any price and suffered any pain for that very moment. In fact, I even felt a profound sense of gratitude for my trials and tribulations. They had served their purpose to stretch and shape me. They had tried my faith and strengthened my faith. Those painful times had indeed paved the way for this very moment of exquisite joy. "After much tribulation come the blessings" (D&C 58:4). We are indeed rich in blessings and we cannot thank Him enough.

I recognize that not everyone will have an experience exactly like ours. You may feel that you don't have anything for which you can feel so profoundly grateful as I did that day in the Nauvoo Temple. You may be still waiting and hoping and praying for your longed-for blessing. You may feel that you are not rich in blessings, but you are! Even our trials and what we don't have, in reality, are blessings. Through the Savior's perfect love and infinite Atonement you and I have blessings unimaginable right here and now, and He promises us the "riches of eternity" (D&C 67:2) hereafter. As King Benjamin declared: "O how you ought to thank your heavenly King!" (Mosiah 2:19). As we thank Him our lives will change. Our burdens may not be immediately lifted, but gratitude will disperse the darkness of discouragement and despondency and replace it with an optimism obtained through faith.

Enter into his gates with thanksgiving, and into his courts with praise: be thankful unto him, and bless his name.

For the Lord is good; his mercy is everlasting; and his truth endureth to all generations.

—Psalm 100:4–5

4

SERVE HIM

THERE IS AN EVENT RECORDED IN THE annals of Church history that I find both inspirational and instructional. From that account there are many lessons to learn and many applications we can make. On Sunday, November 30, 1856, as many of the Saints were holding a Sabbath worship service in the Salt Lake Tabernacle, Brigham Young was informed that the beleaguered survivors of the Martin handcart company were about to enter the Salt Lake Valley. Upon hearing the news, President Young canceled the afternoon worship service and admonished those gathered to go home and prepare to receive and serve these arriving immigrants who had suffered so much.

> The afternoon meeting will be omitted, for I wish the sisters to go home and prepare to give those who have just arrived a mouthful of something to eat, and to wash them and nurse them up. You know that I would give more for a dish of pudding and milk, or a baked potato and salt, were I in the situation of those persons who have just come in, than I would for all your prayers, though you were to stay here all the afternoon and pray. Prayer is

good, but when baked potatoes and pudding and milk are needed, prayer will not supply their place on this occasion; give every duty its proper time and place (*Deseret News,* 10 December 1856, 320; quoted in Andrew D. Olsen, *The Price We Paid,* 399).

I have often thought of this event as a prime example of what Amulek taught in the Book of Mormon and James taught in the New Testament concerning the need for our prayers to be accompanied by acts of charity, service, and compassion. Praying without doing "is vain, and availeth you nothing" (Alma 34:28; see also James 2:14–26).

I came to this conclusion while learning to focus on Christ as I struggled to overcome, or at least deal with, my emotional challenges and debilitating feelings of inadequacy. I learned that no one thing by itself is sufficient. Focusing on Christ involves many things—it requires mind, body, heart, and one's whole soul. In fact, the more I sought to focus on Christ—through prayer, pondering, good thoughts, inspiring music, and profound gratitude—the more I realized that spiritual strength is inseparably linked to serving Him. "For how knoweth a man the master whom he has not served?" King Benjamin asked (Mosiah 5:13). Thinking on Christ and thanking Him requires serving Him. To do otherwise is like all prayers and no potatoes for the starving. Serving our fellowmen, King Benjamin taught us, is indeed serving the Lord (see Mosiah 2:17). In fact, it is the means whereby our worship of and gratitude for the Savior becomes "thanks indeed."

> Because I have been given much, I too must give;
> Because of thy great bounty, Lord, each day I live
> I shall divide my gifts from thee
> With ev'ry brother that I see
> Who has the need of help from me.

> —"Because I Have Been Given Much," *Hymns,* no. 219

Service Leads to Greater Spirituality

"Service is an imperative for true followers of Jesus Christ," Elder Dallin H. Oaks wrote (*Pure in Heart*, 37). I think we all know that—at least in our heads. I must admit, however, that at first glance I viewed Elder Oaks's use of the word *imperative* as one more item on my ever-growing list of "have tos"—a burdensome imperative. I know that was not how he intended it be interpreted. Yet when I am emotionally worn down, the words *service* and *imperative* in the same sentence conjure up images of "projects," "gotta do's," and more demands on my time and emotions. When I am down it is hard to get up for service when I think of it in those terms. In fact, if my experience and the experiences of others with whom I have worked through the years can be generalized, the last thing a person who is suffering from depression and anxiety wants at that difficult time is "imperative" service—which may be viewed through depression-induced distorted thinking as the proverbial straw that breaks the camel's back.

One of the most important lessons that I learned through this struggle, however, was that service is indeed imperative—not only because of what it does for others, but also for what it does for me. Serving the Lord by serving my fellowmen, especially when I may feel least like doing so, is an important means whereby I am saved from my own self-centeredness and the distorted fixation on my own problems, pains, and inadequacies. I have learned that when I serve others—"succor the weak, lift up the hands which hang down, and strengthen the feeble knees" (D&C 81:5)—it is my hands that are lifted up and my knees that are strengthened. No wonder service is "imperative for true followers of Jesus Christ." It is a spiritual and emotional life-preserver—a lifeline that saves us from ourselves.

"When we are engaged in the service of our fellowmen," President

Spencer W. Kimball taught, "not only do our deeds assist them, but we put our own problems in a fresher perspective."

> When we concern ourselves more with others, there is less time to be concerned with ourselves. In the midst of the miracle of serving, there is the promise of Jesus, that by losing ourselves, we find ourselves. (See Matt. 10:39.)
>
> Not only do we "find" ourselves in terms of acknowledging guidance in our lives, but the more we serve our fellowmen in appropriate ways, the more substance there is to our souls. We become more significant individuals as we serve others— indeed, it is easier to "find" ourselves because there is so much more of us to find! ("Small Acts of Service," *Ensign*, December 1974, 2).

I saw this principle in action every day as I worked with our full-time missionaries. Their examples of service constantly inspired and reminded me of what I needed in my own life to have the spiritual strength to faithfully face my own challenges. It is not just for public relations or a "back door" method of finding investigators that full-time missionaries are expected to participate in several hours of community service each week. There are many positive fruits that come from such service, but one of the most significant is the spiritual growth that comes into the lives of the elders and sisters. Service is one of the most powerful antidotes for discouragement. Service builds confidence in one's own abilities.

One particular sister missionary served with us who struggled greatly with depression and anxiety. She would almost fall apart when it was her turn to do a door approach while tracting, talk to a stranger on the street, or teach a lesson. As much as she loved the Lord and the gospel, it was emotionally taxing for her to be a full-time missionary. Her fears and apprehensions created a self-defeating cycle. She would worry herself sick with fear in anticipation of doing the work, then beat herself up emotionally for not doing it as well as she would like, and then become almost paralyzed with guilt afterwards. (I could relate somewhat to what she was going through!) I counseled her, encouraged her, praised her—but nothing I said seemed to help.

Then I noticed something about her—a missionary trait that she didn't even recognize in herself. Even though she felt like she couldn't do many of the traditional missionary activities, she would find some sort of service that she could do. At the homes of investigators and less-active members she and her companion were teaching and fellowshipping, she would mow the lawn, wash the dishes, vacuum the floor, clean the house, rake leaves, or shovel snow from the sidewalk. The others were appreciative of the help, but she was the one blessed—given spiritual strength to carry on with the great challenges she faced as a missionary. I was inspired by her example.

One of the most important responsibilities facing any mission president is to strengthen the spirituality of the missionaries. I found that if I could increase their spirituality many problems would be eliminated and the missionaries would be more effective—because they became more focused on Christ. In interviews when I heard missionaries express feelings of frustration or discouragement, I often assigned them to find ways to do more service. It might be service for a companion, service for an investigator, community service, or just "random acts of kindness."

It never failed—the more they served, the greater their spirituality, the less discouragement they experienced, the more effective they became at finding, and the more power they possessed in teaching and leading. From observing their growth, I desired increased spirituality for myself—not only so that I could lift them up to higher spiritual ground, but also to be able to more effectively deal with my own challenges. What's good for the goose is good for the gander (and goslings)!

At the first of my mission I was overcome by unrelenting expectations of "imperative" service. Yet when I learned to focus on Christ and really serve—even when it was difficult, demanding, and discouraging, and especially when I didn't want to serve—I found that service is imperative to spirituality. There can be no spirituality without service, and spirituality is imperative for strength—a strength in the Lord that bespeaks "I can do all things through Christ which strengtheneth me" (Philippians 4:13). When my focus changed from what I perceived as "imperative" service—just fulfilling my calling—to actually serving Him, my spiritual capacity enlarged, my service became more effective, and my personal happiness increased.

"Why are missionaries happy?" President Gordon B. Hinckley asked. "Because they lose themselves in the service of others. . . . The best antidote I know for worry is work. The best medicine for despair is service. The best cure for weariness is the challenge of helping someone who is even more tired" (*Teachings of Gordon B. Hinckley*, 595–96).

You know what? It works! Service increases spirituality, and spirituality diminishes discouragement and depression. I saw it in action in the lives of our missionaries. But more than that I experienced it in my own life!

Go About Doing Good

Not only did I counsel missionaries who were struggling to engage in more service, but I instructed all the missionaries to do so because of the spiritual effects it had on them individually and on our collective missionary efforts. We often used *Preach My Gospel*, the guide for missionary service, to instruct them to follow the example of the Savior and His disciples in going about doing good (see Acts 10:38; Philippians 2:7). "Many missionaries' experience with service before their missions involved planned 'service projects,' such as helping someone move, serving at a Church farm, or cleaning a yard," the guide states. It instructs them to also become more involved in unplanned or informal service opportunities that arise. "This type of service involves listening to the Spirit to recognize opportunities for small, simple acts of kindness that you can offer to God's children. Pray and be aware of opportunities throughout each day to do good" (*Preach My Gospel*, 168).

Unplanned service opportunities, as well as those planned projects, are valuable not only for full-time missionaries, but for all of us. We all need the spiritual uplift that service affords. The counsel to pray for and be aware of opportunities each day to go about doing good is especially vital for those struggling with emotional challenges. For me, service—be it planned formal service in the Church or community or random acts of kindness and service to family, neighbors, or strangers—is an essential element of therapy that leads to healing and to increased emotional and spiritual strength. It is spiritual medicine that I can't afford not to take. I may not be able to do everything I would like to do, but I can do something to serve others every day. By serving others, I serve Him. This both requires and perpetuates focus on Christ.

Random Acts of Kindness

There is inspiration to be found in the personal examples of random acts of kindness performed by individuals—service rendered not because of some official calling or responsibility they have or "to be seen of men" but because of their inner goodness and charity. The simple, quiet, sometimes even anonymous acts of kindness and compassion bespeak the kind of people we really are and aspire to become.

One of my favorite examples of this was President Howard W. Hunter. Elder Neal A. Maxwell told of an experience he had with President Hunter as they traveled together on a Church assignment to a remote part of the world. Since they shared a hotel room, Elder

Maxwell, who was exhausted from their hectic schedule, asked President Hunter if it would be all right if he took a quick nap before their next appointment. After thirty minutes or so, Elder Maxwell awoke to the image of President Hunter sitting on the edge of his bed polishing Elder Maxwell's shoes. President Hunter was embarrassed that he had been "caught in the act," for he would rather not have had Elder Maxwell even notice what he had done (see "Meek and Lowly," 61). Such a simple (though not so random) act of kindness spoke volumes about President Hunter as a true disciple of Jesus Christ.

From the time I first heard that story, I have tried to look for and take advantage of opportunities to brighten someone else's day with a simple act of service or kindness. I must confess, however, that when I was in the bottom of the pit, emotionally speaking, I didn't rise to the occasion as often as I should have. Random acts of kindness may involve reaching out to random people at random times, but such service doesn't just automatically spring forth. Service takes effort. Service takes thought. Service takes desire. When I was down in the dumps I didn't desire to think about or exert any effort that would stretch me beyond my pity zone (I can't call it a comfort zone because I wasn't comfortable or happy in that zone). I was thinking only of myself and "how bad I have it." In that condition, I was rebuked and called to repentance by the examples of my missionaries and my wife. They didn't say anything to call me to repentance. They didn't have to—their actions reminded me of what I needed to be doing.

There were several times that I received phone calls from strangers thanking me for the unsolicited service and acts of kindness given them by our full-time missionaries. One lady wanted to donate money to the Church because she was so impressed that two young men in suits would stop their own work and help her mow and trim her yard. There was snow shoveling and leaf raking and grocery carrying. The recipients of the random acts of kindness were grateful and impressed, but the real blessing came into the lives of the missionaries who, like the ancient disciples of Christ, "went about doing good." By watching them, I wanted to do better.

When Wendy and I would go for a walk in the neighborhood around the mission home to get some exercise and unwind a little, our walk would almost invariably be interrupted by her stopping to do random acts of kindness. There was the widow who was picking up seed pods that had fallen from her tree who received our help. There was a young family who needed help trimming the broken branches on the large trees in their yard that had been damaged in a severe storm. The mother was trying to help her husband and watch two small children at the same time. I guess I was a little inattentive—thinking about needs in the mission or what we were going to have for dinner—because Wendy gave me a little prodding. "Why don't we help them?" she gently asked. There were many other times when simple, even random, acts of service interrupted the normal flow of our daily routines.

It was not uncommon for Wendy, after a busy and exhausting week of missionary work, to go serve at the food pantry for the poor and homeless in our community. I knew that she felt the stress and pressure of our assignment as much as I did. She missed our children and grandchildren and the comforts of home as much as I did. She battled depression and discouragement, at times as much or more than I did. Yet I often found on the kitchen counter her list of people with special needs in the neighborhood who needed a visit, a phone call, or some other act of service. I would ask her, "How can you do this when you have so much else on your plate?" Her answer was simple, but profound. "It makes me feel better." Random acts of service and kindness when you are on a walk may not be all that conducive to the cardiovascular system, but they are certainly conducive to our spiritual system.

Doing something to help and lift another always lifts our own spirits. Duh! This isn't brain surgery or rocket science. Although a slow learner, I learned that when I am the most "down," if I would do at least one random act of kindness each day—it didn't have to be much and it didn't have to require a lot of time or effort—I always felt better about myself, my challenges, and my life. Every Boy Scout knows the slogan, "Do a good turn daily." Little did I know when I was an eleven-year-old tenderfoot that simply following the Boy Scout slogan of doing a good turn daily would become a powerful antidepressant in my life. What a revolutionary idea! I can see it now—a worldwide campaign—"Random acts of kindness: the new drug of choice."

Service within Families

Several years ago we had a special activity for our family. I told the children that I would be announcing the nature of that activity at our next family home evening. There was great anticipation. There was speculation that Dad would announce that we were going to Disneyland or some other exotic place for our special activity. When the appointed Monday night arrived, I announced that the special activity would be a service project. Disappointed that Disneyland was now out, the children still expressed enthusiasm for a service project. "Where are we going to go?" "Who are we going to serve?" "What are we going to do?" they asked.

"We're not going anywhere," I said. "We're going to stay right here and do service for our family." Our daughter Janey looked at me like I was crazy and then said, "That's not a service project. You can't do service in your own home—that's work!"

My daughter's reaction to the idea of family service typifies a common misconception. We tend to think of loving and serving our fellowmen as being for those outside our immediate view. Yet we often say the most important of the Lord's work that we will ever do is that done within the walls of our own homes. No doubt this involves teaching, leading, and loving, but it also involves serving. "Ye will teach [your children] to walk in the ways of truth and soberness," King Benjamin admonished; "ye will teach them to love one another, and to *serve one another*" (Mosiah 4:15; emphasis added). As with most things, example teaches more effectively than just words.

The family is the laboratory of gospel living. It is where we put into actions what we have learned about in Church. Sometimes it is actually easier to serve strangers, neighbors, or fellow ward members than to serve our families. Even though we may have lots of chores and do lots of things in the home, that is not always the same as family service. One of the all-too-common expressions in our home was, "That's not my job!" Going about doing good—helping others and lifting our own spirits through service—is not compartmentalized by job description.

In talking about service to the family in this context I am not suggesting we do everything for our children, nor am I saying that we shouldn't teach responsibility and self-reliance. What I am suggesting—and what has blessed my life—is that we look for those opportunities within the walls of our own homes to reach beyond ourselves and lift a family member's burden a little. I know it might not be my turn to dump the garbage, but I could sometimes surprise someone by doing it for them. It's a little thing, but it yields big returns. Such little things, especially when done anonymously, will begin to perpetuate themselves and bless the whole family.

Sometimes we may feel overwhelmed, discouraged, even depressed, by all the "have to do's" we face in family responsibilities. I know that. I have faced them myself. What I have experienced, however, is that my emotional outlook improves significantly and my spirituality increases as I strive to render "good turn daily" service at home—an anonymous act of kindness or thoughtfulness that isn't in my normal job description. A daily act of family service may be totally unexpected (in fact, it may send someone into shock), but it will be greatly appreciated, nonetheless, by those we love the most.

Service in the Church

One of the great blessings of Church membership is the opportunity for members to serve in a wide variety of callings. We are often asked to do things that we would not do under normal circumstances—for several reasons: we may not have had any previous experience, or we may not possess a particular talent, or we may not even desire to serve in that capacity. Yet the Lord blesses us with callings and responsibilities that require us to reach beyond ourselves. Faithfulness in our Church callings provides us with life-tutorials that cannot be obtained in any other way. Through service in the Church we bless others and, in turn, we are blessed.

I know that sometimes we may not feel that way. Sometimes we may view callings to serve in the Church as burdens rather than blessings. I have been guilty of that at times. When that happens I have had to spiritually "slap myself upside the head" to change my perspective, repent of my bad attitude, and ask the Lord to help me to serve in the Church for the right reasons. As I have done so, I have come to the realization that service in the Church is a means to an end, not the end itself. Coming to know the Savior is the end that we seek, and service in our respective Church callings paves the way to that end. By serving the flock, we come to know the Good Shepherd.

Throughout the years, as I have listened to the Brethren speak in general conference and as I have seen them in action in a variety of settings, I have learned something about true service in the kingdom. Those who have fully consecrated themselves to the Lord have both a public ministry and a private ministry. Their public ministry is what we usually see—speaking in general conference, presiding and speaking at stake conferences, training leaders, administering the Church, and so on. There is certainly more to do in their public ministry than they have time or energy to accomplish.

However, there is a private ministry that isn't as visible and rarely, if ever, publicized. This kind of service in the Church involves one-on-one contact rather than speaking to and being seen by millions. It involves service that can't be outlined in handbooks or job descriptions. I know of leaders in the Church who, despite their crazy-busy schedules and the heavy load of pressure-packed responsibilities resting upon their shoulders, still find time to visit a widow who is lonely, call someone who is sick and bedridden, or take a troubled teenager to lunch.

There are thoughtful letters and notes to those in need. There is the anonymous gift of a white shirt and tie to a deacon whose family could not afford to buy them. The examples of such private-ministry service are myriad. Although perhaps unnoticed by the Church or world in general, these acts are always noticed by the beneficiaries and by Him whose witness the Brethren are.

When our family lived in Israel, President James E. Faust and his beloved wife, Ruth, came on an assignment to the BYU Jerusalem Center. They were accompanied by Elder Jeffrey R. Holland and his wife, Pat. They spoke at the district conference, at a fireside for the students, and at a reception for prominent and influential people from Israel. It was part of their official assignment—their public ministry.

It was the private ministry, however, that our family will never forget. Unbeknownst to me, our nine-year-old daughter, Janey, asked her mother to bake cookies and then secretly delivered them to the Fausts and Hollands. Each plate of cookies held a note written in her crooked penmanship that read "From the Cookie Monster." Janey placed the surprise in front of each apartment door, rang the doorbell, and ran away. She wanted her gift of service to be anonymous.

Late that evening, as we were watching a movie and eating popcorn, a knock came at our apartment door. "Come on in," I yelled, thinking it was some of our students coming to join us. In walked President and Sister Faust and Elder and Sister Holland. We were shocked and a little embarrassed, since we were all in our pajamas or sweats and our mouths were full of popcorn.

"I just came to see the Cookie Monster," President Faust announced. It took a minute for us to figure out what he was talking about. At first, he didn't want us to awaken Janey, who had already gone to bed. But this was something I didn't want her to miss—a personal visit from two Apostles of the Lord. There were hugs and expressions of love and appreciation for a sleepy nine-year-old. No doubt it had been a long, busy, exhausting day for our visitors, but they still sought out a little girl to thank and to love. That simple act of a private ministry probably has meant more to our daughter than almost anything those brethren have said or done in their public ministry.

We strengthen and are strengthened through service in the Church. We are blessed by fulfilling our callings as home and visiting teachers, teachers of classes, leaders in quorums and auxiliaries, or even as Cubmaster. Just as our callings differ, so do our individual capacities and circumstances. You may be a mission president one week and a sacrament meeting door greeter the next. It doesn't matter where we serve, but how—but most of all that we serve.

I hear the question asked at times, "What are you doing in the Church?" More than once I have heard people say, "I don't have a calling right now." We generally equate callings to "serving in the Church." I have to confess, however, that there have been times that I fulfilled my calling, but I didn't really serve.

On the other hand, I know of a woman who, because of her serious illness, was not able to hold a formal Church calling. Yet she went about doing good in many ways. She couldn't leave her home, but she could pray. She could call the temple and put the names of sick ward members on the prayer roll. She did family history name-extraction work. She wrote to missionaries. All who came to serve her felt like she was serving them with her joy, faith, and optimism. She was serving in significant ways—even though she didn't think she was.

Another young mother I know served despite difficult challenges. Because of the lingering effects of her emotional breakdown, she could not handle a demanding Church calling, but she served in other significant ways. She helped out in the nursery. She signed up for one-time service assignments at the cannery, family history library, or temple. She was able to do these things because she knew that by so doing she would feel better and her strength would increase. Certainly her efforts to serve when she was weak made her stronger. She later served as a Relief Society president. No doubt her simple acts of private-ministry service, when she wasn't emotionally strong, enabled and empowered her later public-ministry service.

Each of us can, likewise, have a private ministry regardless of our callings. In fact, that ministry is just as important, if not more so, than the more visible things we do in our official callings. We will be emotionally enlarged and spiritually strengthened if we will look for small ways to serve in the Church. You don't have to be the bishop or the Relief Society president to serve. Every smile or encouraging word is also an act of service. No matter how small or how large the giving may be, if given in love and with real intent, it will be abundantly rewarded by Him whose supreme service saves us all.

"All That You Do for Them, You Do for Me"

Sister Top recounted a story to every new group of missionaries that arrived in our mission. It has been one of her favorites for many years. She used the story to remind the missionaries that they represent Jesus

Christ in very deed. We could not have known at the first of our mission what the story would later come to mean to us.

Willard Bean and his wife, Rebecca, married in the Manti Temple on September 14, 1914. Less than six months later, the newlyweds were called and set apart by President Joseph Fielding Smith for a special assignment to go to Palmyra, New York. They were to live in the Joseph Smith home that the Church had recently purchased. The Beans would be the first Latter-day Saints to live in the area since the early Saints were driven out in 1831. Their mission was to help break down the prejudices of the people and to prepare the way for future missionary work in that area.

They expected their mission to last only a few years. Instead, it spanned a quarter of a century. They arrived in New York as newlyweds and departed as grandparents. Their contributions to missionary work, establishing branches of the Church, and improving relationships with the people over that period of time are monumental. These successes came, however, after much opposition and difficulty. Under the direction of the Eastern States mission president, Willard presided over local Church meetings and worked with the full-time missionaries that would later be sent to that area. Sometimes the demands of the assignment were almost unbearable, particularly for Rebecca. She not only had responsibilities for missionaries and Church members, but also for the nurture and care of a growing young family. It was within this context that she had what she later referred to as "the most wonderful experience" while living and serving in Palmyra. She recounted:

> It was a hot summer day, and we had had a lot of visitors that day. It had been a hard day for me. I had a baby just a year old, and I had carried him around on my arm most of the day to get my work done. I was too warm. Everything had gone against us. Night time came and we had had lunch for our

visitors and supper at night and I had put my children to bed. We had a nice evening with housework all done.

Dr. [James E.] Talmage and some missionaries were there, and we had a wonderful evening talking together. They all seemed tired, so I took them upstairs and showed them where they could sleep.

When I came down, I decided to pick up a few things and make things easier for myself in the morning. But I was so weary and so tired that I was crying a little as I straightened things around. Everybody was in bed and asleep but me. I looked at the clock and it was 11:00, and I can remember so well that I said, "I better call it a day."

I went into my room and my husband and my baby were sound asleep. It was peaceful and quiet. I got myself ready for bed, and I was crying on my pillow. Then this dream or vision came to me.

I thought it was another day. It had been a wonderful morning. I had prepared breakfast for my visitors. My children were happily playing around. I had done my work and cared for the baby, and he was contented and happy. Then I prepared lunch. I called our visitors in to lunch, and we were all seated around the table. My little baby was in his high chair, and everything was just peaceful and wonderful and sweet.

There was a knock on the front door. I went in and opened it, and there was a very handsome young man standing there. I just took it for granted that he was just another new missionary that had come to see us. I said, "You're here just in time for lunch. Come with me."

As he walked through the little hall into the dining room, I noticed he put some pamphlets down on the little table there. We walked into the dining room, and I introduced him around and then I said, "Now, you sit right here by Dr. Talmage, and I'll set a plate for you."

I thought, of course, that he was strange to all of us, and yet he and Dr. Talmage seemed so happy to see each other. They talked about such wonderful things while we were eating. Some of them we could hardly understand. The spirit and mood present there was so peaceful and nice, and everyone seemed so happy to be together.

After the meal was over, Dr. Talmage said to the missionary, "Now, let's go outside and just be alone and enjoy the spirit of this wonderful place because," he said, "you'll soon have to leave."

I put my baby to bed and the other little ones went out to play, and then I was alone with this young man. He thanked me for having him to dinner and told me how much it meant for him to be there. He told me that he thought that the children were so sweet and well trained, and I felt so happy about that.

And then we walked in the hall together, and he said, "I have far to go so I must be on my way."

I turned from him for just a moment to pick up the little pamphlets that he had put on the table; and when I turned back to him it was the Savior who stood before me, and He was in His glory. I could not tell you the love and the sweetness that He had in His face and in His eyes. Lovingly He laid His hands on my shoulders, and He looked down into my face with the kindest face that I have ever seen. And this is what He said to me:

"Sister Bean, this day hasn't been too hard for you, has it?"

I said, "Oh, no, I have been so happy with my work and everything has gone so well."

Then He said, "I promise you if you will go about your work every day as you have done it this day, you will be equal to it. Remember these missionaries represent me on this earth and all you do unto them, you do unto me."

And I know I was crying as we walked through the hall out onto the porch. He repeated the same thing: "These missionaries represent me on earth, and all you do unto them, you do unto me."

Then He started upward. The roof of the porch was no obstruction for Him to go through nor for me to see through. He went upward and upward and upward. I wondered and wondered how I could see Him so far away. And then all at once He disappeared, and I was crying on my pillow like I was when I went to bed (in *Willard Bean, the Fighting Parson,* 80–83).

In her later life, Rebecca Bean often bore testimony of how the Savior's love at that difficult time had removed all frustration from her life and how she was given strength to endure any difficulty and face any challenge. As Wendy would share that story with those newly arrived missionaries—elders and sisters who were already homesick, scared, anxious, a little overwhelmed and worried—I saw them as the Lord saw them. I started to really understand the Savior's words to Rebecca Bean: "These missionaries represent me on this earth and all you do for them, you do for me." Those words hit me like a ton of bricks! How in the world could I be so depressed and discouraged, so pitiful and pathetic, if I really believed that? No amount of service to the Lord could adequately express my appreciation and adoration. I knew I was "an unprofitable servant"—totally dependent upon the Lord. I thought I had faith in Christ, but Rebecca Bean's "vision" opened my eyes. I realized that I hadn't been exercising that faith as much as I could have. I saw how the Savior's perfect love can destroy despair, discouragement, and depression. Moreover, I came to understand that the more I serve, the more I will feel that love.

Rebecca Bean's experience is certainly relevant for mission presidents, but it isn't just about caring for missionaries as servants of the Lord. It is relevant for all of us. It is about serving and caring for others—family, friends, neighbors, and even strangers. They are all God's children—our literal brothers and sisters. What we do for them, we do for Him. What He does for us in return "surpasses all understanding" (D&C 76:89).

> *Herein is love, not that we loved God, but that he loved us, and sent his Son to be the propitiation for our sins.*
>
> *Beloved, if God so loved us, we ought also to love one another. . . .*
>
> *And this commandment have we from him, That he who loveth God love his brother also.*
>
> —1 John 4:10–11, 21

5

LEARN OF HIM

IN MAY 2007, NOLA OCHS GRADUATED from Fort Hays State University in Kansas. Nola is not unique in donning cap and gown to march in a graduation processional to receive the much coveted diploma as family and friends adoringly look on. Literally, tens of thousands receive their college degrees each year in the United States alone. What is unique about Nola, however, is that she is ninety-five years old—the world's oldest college graduate. It was also rather unique that graduating with her was her twenty-one-year-old granddaughter. Nola's thirty-five year quest for a college degree was driven by her love for learning, not by her need for a career. "I like to study and learn," she said. "It gives me a sense of satisfaction."

Nola may be the oldest college graduate in the world, but there are many like her who value education and continue to learn and accomplish even in old age. I have participated in many commencement exercises at Brigham Young University through the years, and at each the oldest graduate is introduced and honored. (When I was struggling to pass a required statistics course in order to get my degree I was afraid that I would actually become that oldest graduate!) Laird Snelgrove became the oldest BYU graduate at ninety-one years old when he received his degree in Spanish in December 2002. What an accomplishment!

There certainly have been many others who, though not record-breaking or recognized publicly, continue their education throughout their lives because of the satisfaction that accompanies learning. I have had students in their eighties and nineties attend classes that I teach. I learn more from them than I teach them. One elderly sister who faithfully attended class, even though she was bent over with age and arthritis and walked only with assistance, declared: "If I stop learning, I'll stop living!" That simple statement inspires me.

As Latter-day Saints, we believe that education is for eternity. Learning blesses our lives here and hereafter. We are commanded by the Lord to "seek ye out of the best books words of wisdom" and to continually seek learning of things both spiritual and temporal (see D&C 88:118; also verses 78–80). Schools, classes, books, and libraries are part of our divine, as well as our pioneer, heritage. Learning should be as much a spiritual quest as it is an intellectual one.

"When all is said and done, we are all students," President Gordon B. Hinckley taught. "If the day ever comes when we quit learning, look out. We will just atrophy and die."

There is a great potential within each of us to go on learning. Regardless of our age, unless there be serious illness, we can read, study, drink in the writings of wonderful men and women. . . .

We must go on growing. We must continuously learn. It is a divinely given mandate that we go on adding to our knowledge.

We have access to institute classes, extension courses,

education weeks, and many other opportunities where, as we study and match our minds with others, we will discover a tremendous reservoir of capacity within ourselves (*Teachings of Gordon B. Hinckley,* 302–3).

There are many benefits from a continual quest for knowledge. Some are obvious and others are not. Some are temporal in nature and others are spiritual. Each contributes to our spiritual strength and intellectual capacity. In modern revelation, the Lord declared that "the glory of God is intelligence, or, in other words, *light* and *truth*" (D&C 93:36; emphasis added) and commanded us to "seek learning, even by *study* and also by *faith*" (D&C 88:118; emphasis added). For me, these passages speak of both the means and the ends of learning. It appears to me that the Lord is saying that intelligence—God's knowledge and glory, which is light and truth—at least for us on earth, is both temporal and spiritual.

Acquiring that intelligence requires both intellectual and spiritual means—study, pondering, faith, prayer, and worthy living. In the end, the blessings and benefits of such learning, including what President Hinckley called "a tremendous reservoir of capacity," will also be temporal and spiritual, earthly and eternal.

In one of the most familiar passages in the New Testament, Jesus teaches us about a specific kind of learning and what that learning will yield in our lives. "Come unto me, all ye that labour and are heavy laden, and I will give you rest," the Lord promised. "Take my yoke upon you, and *learn of me;* for I am meek and lowly in heart: and *ye shall find rest unto your souls*" (Matthew 11:28–29; emphasis added).

This passage has particular relevance to me. I know from personal experience that for someone in the depths of depression, the promise of personal peace and rest is heartening and hopeful. The words *labour* and *heavy laden* have emotional and spiritual dimensions as much as physical. Surely those who struggle with anxiety and depression "labour" in a very real way. Those who carry emotional burdens like perfectionism, discouragement, or self-contempt are truly "heavy laden." The Savior's invitation is especially applicable to them. Without His promise of "rest unto your souls," it would be easy to give up and give in to despair.

"Learn of me," Jesus declared. He didn't just say, "Take a physics class." (No offense intended to physicists or those who like physics.) Continuing education—whether it be in physics or family history, geology or geometry—has its place and will bless our lives in many, many ways. There is no doubt about that. The Lord has indeed commanded us to learn as much as we can about all that we can. Learning is its own reward.

What Jesus is specifically talking about, however, is that kind of knowledge—learning of Him—that not only increases the intellect, but also heals the heart, soothes the soul, strengthens the spirit, and expands the character. All of this in turn fills our "reservoir of capacity."

The word *disciple* means a learner or pupil (see Bible Dictionary, 657). Jesus is the Master Teacher. We are His students. If we are to be His disciples—in the truest sense of that word—we must sit at His feet, figuratively speaking, and learn of Him. We must learn those things that He would have us know, so that we can do the things He would have us do, so that we can become what He would have us become. He has provided the curriculum and specific means whereby we learn of Him— means that can keep us spiritually "on task," continually focused on Him and His strengthening and saving grace.

"The Pleasing Word of God"

President Spencer W. Kimball admitted that at times in his life he felt distanced from God—"that no divine ear is listening and no divine voice is speaking." All of us face similar moments. That is part and parcel of the mortal experience—part of the requisite test of faith. Unfortunately, some of us don't avail ourselves of President Kimball's prescription for curing low spirituality levels—a prescription with little danger of overdose. "If I immerse myself in the scriptures," he testified, "the distance narrows and the spirituality returns" (*Teachings of Spencer W. Kimball,* 135).

One of the most significant ways we learn of Him and focus on Him is conscientious study of the scriptures—"feasting upon the word of Christ" as Nephi described it (see 2 Nephi 31:20). This is particularly true for those who struggle with self-worth issues, feelings of insecurity and inadequacy, discouragement, despondency, and other emotional challenges. "The pleasing word of God," the Book of Mormon prophet Jacob declared, "healeth the wounded soul" (Jacob 2:8).

As a religious educator, I study the scriptures for a living. My career has allowed me time and resources to study in depth all of the standard works of the Church. I have been able to teach all of the scripture courses and other courses in Latter-day Saint theology and history. My professional passion has been for the scriptures. I feel as Nephi of old: "My soul delighteth in the scriptures, . . . and my heart pondereth continually upon [them]" (2 Nephi 4:15–16). It is a wonderful career, and sometimes I feel guilty being paid to study and teach the scriptures (but not so guilty as to give up my salary).

There are occupational hazards, however—and I'm not talking about the risks of paper cuts from turning pages. Let me explain. Most of my scripture study effort through the years has been directed to developing study guides and lectures for my classes, researching for writing projects, or preparing talks. I try to think deeply about the scriptures in order to gain new insights and applications from them. These efforts have served me well—at least professionally and intellectually (although some may argue that point).

I have found, however, that "searching" the scriptures in preparation for a talk or lesson is not the same as "feasting" upon the words of Christ for personal growth and spirituality. I need to learn *of* Him and not just learn *about* Him. I need to feel Him deep within my soul, not just know chapter and verse. Sometimes my personal scripture study could be characterized as getting through the scriptures instead of getting the scriptures through to me.

The limitations of this approach became painfully manifest while I served as mission president and struggled with my inadequacies and emotional challenges. I discovered that, in my duress, my years of lesson-preparing scripture study may have helped in teaching the missionaries at zone conferences, but they were not adequate to "heal" my "wounded soul." When "forced" to my knees, I needed to learn of Him right then to partake of His promised peace. To be spiritually strengthened and sustained, I needed renewed scripture "feasting." I couldn't rely on past study for pressing personal needs any more than a sumptuous Thanksgiving dinner eaten ten years ago can satisfy my present hunger.

"Try the virtue of the word of God" became a guiding philosophy in our efforts to strengthen the spirituality of the missionaries with whom we served. It was Alma's example in preaching the word of God to the apostate Zoramites that inspired us to more effectively utilize the power of the scriptures.

> And now, as the preaching of the word had a great tendency to lead the people to do that which was just—yea, it had had more powerful effect upon the minds of the people than the sword, or anything else, which had happened unto them— therefore Alma thought it was expedient that they should try the virtue of the word of God (Alma 31:5).

We saw a "mighty change" in the lives of individual missionaries and in the success of the entire mission as we studied and taught more from the scriptures. I would say it was a miraculous transformation, but it really wasn't a miracle, just a fulfillment of what the scriptures themselves promise. I not only saw the power of the word in others' lives, I began to experience that power in a new way in my own. Alma's words took on a new meaning to me—a "more powerful effect upon the minds of the people than the sword, or anything else." The virtue, or power, of the scriptures can change behaviors and fortify faith, but it also has the power to elevate one's thinking and change attitudes. As we learn of Him our minds are powerfully and positively affected. Faith can displace fears. Feasting upon the words of Christ draws us nearer to Him.

One particular scripture activity had a profound impact on my faith, spirituality, and confidence as I struggled with my doubts and discouragement. I had given a new, unmarked copy of the Book of Mormon to each missionary, along with some colored pencils. They were given the assignment to look for and mark specific doctrines in their daily personal and companion study. It was a remarkable experience—for the entire mission collectively and for me personally.

One of the assigned topics was the Atonement of Jesus Christ. I have studied and taught and written much on that topic before, but with this project I learned much more than I could have imagined. Influenced by the challenges and concerns that I was then experiencing, my personal scripture study led to new learning—new insights, feelings, and strength from the Spirit of the Lord. I came to experience in a profoundly personal way what President Ezra Taft Benson taught concerning scripture study in general and the Book of Mormon in particular:

> Many a man in his hour of trial has turned to the Book of Mormon and been enlightened, enlivened, and comforted. The psalms in the Old Testament have a special food for the soul of one in distress. In our day we are blessed with the Doctrine and

Covenants, modern revelation. . . . [These] are crucial reading and can give direction and comfort in an hour when one is down (*The Teachings of Ezra Taft Benson,* 40).

It is not just that the Book of Mormon teaches us truth, though it indeed does that. It is not just that the Book of Mormon bears testimony of Christ, though it indeed does that, too. But there is something more. There is a power in the book which will begin to flow into your lives the moment you begin a serious study of the book. . . . The scriptures are called "the words of life" (see D&C 84:85), and nowhere is that more true than it is of the Book of Mormon. When you begin to hunger and thirst after those words, you will find life in greater and greater abundance (*A Witness and a Warning,* 21–22).

I often hear people complain about studying the scriptures. "I don't read well" or "I don't get anything out of it" or "I don't understand what I read," they protest. Even some of our full-time missionaries, who have two hours set aside each day for study, view scripture study as a chore. It isn't so much about reading comprehension or intellectual understanding as it is about faith and willingness to receive the "power of the word." Whether we are gospel scholars or scripture novices, studying the scriptures blesses our lives. Even when we don't understand everything we read, we are still being infused with spiritual strength and power. Faithful study of scriptures, especially when we may feel down in the dumps, enhances our spiritual sensitivities. Feeling is sometimes more valuable than understanding.

After delivering a lecture about the Book of Mormon many years ago, I talked at the podium with an elderly couple who desired to share an experience. What they shared with me touched my heart and has never left me. They told of how they had tried to study the scriptures, particularly the Book of Mormon, every day with their family. As any parent who has sought to do the same thing knows, it can be difficult. After all but one of their children were grown and out of the nest, the parents decided that they didn't need to continue their morning practice of family scripture study. The one remaining child—now an adult—was mentally handicapped. Assuming he got nothing out of their scripture study, they ceased the practice with the intention of spending more time on their own personal study. However, the handicapped son, with his limited communication skills, said, "Don't stop reading to me. I like the way it makes me feel."

He didn't know how profound his statement was. Truly, as we seek to learn of Christ by studying His words, we will feel something akin to what Jeremiah described as "a burning fire shut up in my bones" (Jeremiah 20:9). Like a comforting fire on a cold night, the "pleasing word of God" can warm any soul chilled by life's many challenges. When I was down and emotionally cold, studying the scriptures—not because I was preparing a talk or a zone conference presentation, but because I needed strength for myself—brought warmth, and I liked the way it made me feel.

"Whether by Mine Own Voice or by the Voice of My Servants, It Is the Same"

At the organization of the Church on April 6, 1830, the Lord commanded that "the several elders composing this church . . . are to meet in conference" on a regular basis (see D&C 20:61–62). While conferences "do whatever church business is necessary to be done," as the revelation directs, their primary purpose is deeply spiritual. The fruits, or blessings, of general conference are likewise spiritual in nature, profoundly affecting both the individual and the institution. They provide us with another valuable means whereby we can learn of Him—one of the Lord's ways whereby He instructs His people. As He himself stated, "whether by mine own voice or by the voice of my servants, it is the same" (D&C 1:38).

I have always loved general conference and have appreciated the blessing it is to hear the testimonies and teachings of the Lord's anointed servants. My parents told me that when I was but a toddler I would watch intently the broadcast of general conference on our old black-and-white television. When President David O. McKay would appear on the screen, they said, I would kiss the television and say, "I love him." Though I may not kiss the television screen anymore, I still love the prophets and apostles and cherish listening to their counsel. General conference is to me like a lush oasis is to a desert traveler—a refreshing respite amidst a difficult journey, a time of renewal of strength, a renewal of direction and determination.

"Conference time is a season of spiritual revival," taught President Howard W. Hunter, "when knowledge and testimony are increased and solidified that God lives and blesses those who are faithful . . .—a time when souls are stirred and resolutions are made to be better husbands and wives, fathers and mothers, more obedient sons and daughters, better friends and neighbors" ("Conference Time," *Ensign,* November 1981, 12).

General conference always seems to come right when my spiritual and emotional "batteries" are running the lowest. Have you felt that way too? Do you also find that your spiritual "batteries" are recharged by the messages delivered and the spirit that attends the sessions? I do. That is why I love general conference so much. There have been many, many times when I felt that the speaker was talking only to me—giving personal counsel and comfort that I desperately needed at that moment. Perhaps you have had that experience as well. Sometimes it is as if the Savior Himself is teaching a class of one—me. In fact, He is—"whether by mine own voice or by the voice of my servants, it is the same."

This was particularly true when I was presiding over a mission and after I had experienced my breakdown. The spiritual oasis afforded by conference at that difficult and demanding time of my life was probably more appreciated and the messages more applied than at any other time. In my emotionally weakened condition, I feared that I would be "sent over the edge" by talks that would highlight my spiritual inadequacy, remind me of my sins, call me to repentance, and then emphatically add to my growing list of "oughta do's."

While I was certainly reminded of things that needed more of my spiritual focus, the spirit of general conference was one of building up, not beating down. Listening to the Lord's servants, like learning at the feet of the Savior, is an experience in love, lifting, hope, and healing. More than at any other time in my life, the messages of general conference inspired and instructed me. I am quite sure that it was not because the talks were just better during those three years. I am convinced that because of my personal needs—the challenges I faced, the problems I encountered, and the responsibilities on my shoulders—general conference became a veritable "fountain of living waters" (1 Nephi 11:25) to which I could go for refreshment again and again and again.

What a blessing it is for each of us to live in this day and age when we can drink from that fountain any time we desire! With all of the technology that is available, we can have almost immediate access to the words of the Lord's servants. We can read their words. We can listen to their talks. We can watch them. We can continually be blessed by and learn from those who are called to represent the Master—"to stand in his place; to say and do what he himself would say and do if he personally were ministering among the very people to whom [they are sent]" (Elder Bruce R. McConkie, "My Commission," in *The Bruce R. McConkie Story,* 215). No wonder prophets have declared that the messages of general conference should "stand next to your standard works and be referred to frequently" (*The Teachings of Ezra Taft Benson,* 333) and be "the guide to [your] walk and talk during the next six months" (*The Teachings of Harold B. Lee,* 469).

To the early Saints the Lord declared:

> Behold, thus saith the Lord unto you my servants, it is expedient in me that the elders of my church should be called together, from the east and from the west, and from the north and from the south, by letter or some other way.
>
> And it shall come to pass, that inasmuch as they are faithful, and exercise faith in me, I will pour out my Spirit upon them in the day that they assemble themselves together.
>
> And it shall come to pass that they shall go forth into the regions round about, and preach repentance unto the people.
>
> And *many shall be converted,* insomuch that ye shall obtain power to organize yourselves according to the laws of man;
>
> That your enemies may not have power over you; that you may be preserved in all things (D&C 44:1–5; emphasis added).

It is the same for us today. I am a beneficiary of the Lord's promise. I have experienced the spiritual outpouring associated with general conference many times. Yet this scripture took on even greater meaning to me in another setting. At one of our annual area mission presidents (and wives) conferences, we were privileged to have Elder Richard G. Scott of the Quorum of the Twelve as our General Authority visitor. He spoke to us several times and provided important training. Although I took several pages of notes, I must confess that today I don't remember much of what he taught in the training.

However, I will never forget his closing testimony. As a special witness of the Lord Jesus Christ, he bore powerful witness of the living Christ and the power of His Atonement; his words were accompanied by apostolic authority and sure knowledge. I have never felt anything like it. My heart burned within me. The power of his witness penetrated every fiber of my being. I cannot adequately describe in words what he said and what I felt.

Suffice it to say, at that sacred moment, I knew that Elder Scott knew. I didn't have to see the resurrected Lord to know with absolute surety, because the Spirit so powerfully confirmed that fact. As Elder Scott bore his apostolic witness I knew that I too know! I am not a special witness like Elder Scott, but accompanying his words a powerful, even special, witness came to me. I, and undoubtedly all the other people in that room, experienced what Doctrine and Covenants 44 describes—the Spirit had indeed been poured out upon us and we were converted, or, more accurately, "reconverted." Each of us was spiritually strengthened and empowered to magnify our callings, to lift our missionaries to greater spiritual heights, and to more effectively proclaim the gospel to our respective parts of the world. With faith like David, we were ready to take on any Goliath.

For me, however, I left with something more. The phrase "that your enemies may not have power over you; that you may be preserved in all things" became clear. I understood that the Lord, through His servants, offers me power over my enemies. The enemy is not just powers of darkness, wickedness, temptation, persecution, or opposition to the work. My own personal enemies that seek to derail my spiritual focus include discouragement, depression, anxiety, fear, and debilitating feelings of inadequacy. I need all the help I can get in battling these enemies. The Lord's offer of power over my enemies stands. I just need to take Him at His word.

How grateful I am that the words of living prophets and apostles can fortify my faith, strengthen my spirituality, and lift me up when I am down. I left that conference forever changed. The challenges remained. The enemies still gathered. I still had to face the fight, but I was infused with a renewed sense of protection and power. From the Christlike love I felt from Elder Scott, his inspired counsel, the special witness he bore, and an apostolic blessing he pronounced, I left with an absolute assurance that I could face life's challenges and difficulties, because the Lord means what He says: "Whatsoever [the Lord's servants] shall speak when moved upon by the Holy Ghost shall be scripture, shall be the will of the Lord, shall be the mind of the Lord, shall be the word of the Lord, shall be the voice of the Lord, and the power of God unto salvation" (D&C 68:4).

"A House of Learning, a House of Glory"

Several years ago Wendy and I joined a few couples from our ward for an excursion to the Mesa Temple. We were living in Snowflake, Arizona, at the time. With a three-hour drive ahead of us, we departed long before sunrise to make it to the temple in time for our assignment. As we came down from the mountains into the valley, the sun was just beginning its ascent over the eastern hills. It wasn't quite dark anymore, but it wasn't light yet either.

Off in the distance we could see something in the road. In this twilight between night and day, it was an eerie sight. As we approached closer we could see it was a person standing in the middle of the road. What started as just eerie became surreal, even frightening. The man standing in the road was covered in blood. He stated that he had been in a car accident, that his friend was still in the car, and that he needed our help in getting him out of the car. There was no car anywhere in sight. "It's over that ridge," the man said, pointing out into the desert.

The wives stayed in the van as the husbands followed the injured man. Now maybe I've seen too many horror movies in my day (one is too many in my estimation), because my heart was beating out of my chest as I expected some hockey-masked crazed killer with an axe in his hand to jump out from behind the bushes. As we walked over the ridge we caught our first glimpse of a car on its roof with smoke coming out of the engine. It was clear that the vehicle had left the highway at a very high speed, had rolled, and had crashed into the trees.

We extricated the seriously injured passenger and got both men back to the highway. Our wives immediately jumped into action with pillows, blankets, and comforting reassurances. This was in the day before everyone had cell phones, so we were in a quandary as to how we were going to call for an ambulance. We were right smack in the middle of nowhere—thirty miles from the closest town. Just then another couple from the ward drove up. Providentially, their car was equipped with a CB radio, and the wife was a registered nurse. The ambulance was called. Prayers were offered, both silently and vocally. We did the best we could and then waited and waited.

It seemed like it took forever for the ambulance to arrive, but it was probably only about a half hour. We had all been so busily involved in administering first aid that time stood still and thoughts of our temple assignment were shoved to the back of our minds.

After the ambulance had sped away, we resumed our journey, but it was hard to gather our thoughts and refocus on the temple. My heart pounded and my hands trembled from the adrenaline rush. We had been through quite an ordeal, and we couldn't quickly or easily shift gears—mentally, emotionally, or spiritually. When we finally arrived at the temple, we were all grateful that we had missed our session. (Being the impatient, natural man that I am, I confess that I'm normally anything but grateful when I miss a session and must wait a few minutes or an hour.) We dressed in white and quietly sat in the chapel waiting for the next session.

It was at that moment that I realized as never before the blessing of the house of the Lord as a place where we leave worldly concerns behind and learn of Him. The peace, quiet, and tranquility of that holy place stood in striking contrast to the craziness we had just been through. I knew it before, but on that day I experienced it in a unique and unforgettable way—the temple is heaven on earth, a place where those who enter "may feel [God's] power, and feel constrained to acknowledge that . . . it is [God's] house, a place of [His] holiness" (D&C 109:13; see also D&C 97:12–16).

The temple is central to our worship of the Lord Jesus Christ—both individually and institutionally. It is not only a place where sacred ordinances are performed and forever families are created. It is a place of sacred communion, where we on the earth can touch eternity—"a house of prayer, . . . a house of faith, a house of learning, a house of glory, a house of order" (D&C 88:119; see also D&C 109:6–21). Finding peace to our souls requires learning of Him, and there is no greater place on earth where such learning can occur than in the house of the Lord. Just as we can hear the voice of the Lord through the scriptures and the words of living prophets, we can also hear and feel His words when we are in His house.

Elder John A. Widtsoe taught:

> Temple work . . . gives a wonderful opportunity for keeping alive our spiritual knowledge and strength. . . . The mighty perspective of eternity is unraveled before us in the holy temples; . . . and the drama of eternal life is unfolded before us. Then I see more clearly my place amidst the things of the universe, my place among the purposes of God; I am better able to place myself where I belong, and I am better able to value and to weigh, to separate and to organize the common, ordinary duties of my life, *so that the little things shall not oppress me or take away my vision of the greater things God has given me* (in Conference Report, April 1922, 97–98; emphasis added).

Obtaining and maintaining this eternal perspective is vital as we all grapple with the normal pressures of life. We all need that perspective when we encounter discouragement and disappointment. We all have our share of insecurities. Every family is dysfunctional and every person has flaws in some way or another—because we are mortals. For some, however, there are serious struggles with out-of-the-ordinary emotional challenges. I fall into all of those categories. As a result, I have learned that the temple is a place where I can leave behind the "baggage" and feel the Lord's loving, guiding, strengthening, and peace-giving influence. I may not learn any new or cosmic mystery each time I go to the temple, but I always learn and relearn who I am and what matters most. I always feel peace. I always feel the Savior's love. All of these things combine, as Elder Widtsoe taught, "so that the little things shall not oppress me or take away my vision of the greater things God has given me." That is what learning of Him in His house does for me.

One of the things that most wore on me when I served as mission president was the non-stop nature of the assignment. At times I felt like I was strapped to a carousel pony on a high-speed merry-go-round with no way to get off. There was always somewhere to go, someone to see, and something that must be done. I was always "on call." My cell phone seemed like it was an actual anatomical appendage. There was no escape—at least for three years!

I may be overstating it a tad, but I want you to understand why the temple became such a vital venue of refuge and refreshment—spiritually, emotionally, and physically. No phone calls. No interviews. No meetings. No deadlines. No problems—at least no problems that I could do anything about for a few hours. I cannot overstate how much the temple came to be a place of peace, a place of revelation, a place of rest and rejuvenation—a place of learning of and listening to Him.

"Beside the Still Waters"

C. S. Lewis insightfully observed: "God wants to give us something, but cannot, because our hands are full—there's nowhere for Him to put it" (*The Problem of Pain,* 96). If I could amplify and update Lewis's words, I would say: "God wants to say something to us, but we can't hear Him—because the kids are screaming, we're on the phone, plugged into an iPod, distracted by personal problems, have ADHD, or all of the above."

We live in a world with all kinds of noise—external and internal. Our busy lives, our high-tech toys (some prefer to call them tools), and the ubiquitous background noise of modern society are but a few examples of the external noise that prevent us from hearing the Lord and learning of Him. In addition, internal noise comes in the form of worries and woes that rattle around in our heads, creating such an emotional clatter we cannot comprehend His words and will for us. When I desire to hear His voice, feel His spirit, and learn of Him—especially when I am discouraged, depressed, and desperately in need of strength—I have to make extra time and exert extra effort to meditate. I am not talking about yoga meditation, hypnotic concentration, or visualization exercises, though each of these may be helpful for some. You can call it what you like—focusing, pondering, "zoning out," "time out," quiet time, "minute vacations," or "going to my happy place." In my own life I have learned (mostly the hard way) that meditation—taking time to think and feel deeply—is as vital to my emotional and spiritual well-being as proper nutrition and exercise is to my physical health.

When we relentlessly drive ourselves—often unmercifully—we tend to feel guilty for taking time for ourselves. We may think of it as doing nothing. Meditation, however, is not doing nothing. It is doing something spiritually significant. It is hard work to think deeply, to listen intently, and to feel spiritually.

"We need the Spirit of the Lord in our lives more," President Gordon B. Hinckley observed:

We live in a very mad world when all is said and done. The pressures are tremendous. We fly at high speeds. We drive at high speeds. We program ourselves. . . . There is hardly time to reflect and think and pause and meditate. I daresay that most [of us] have not taken an hour in the last year to just sit down quietly, each man [or woman] to himself [or herself], as a son [or daughter] of God, reflecting upon his [or her] place in this world, upon his [or her] destiny, upon his [or her] capacity to do good, upon his [or her] mission to make some changes for good. We need to. . . . President McKay said to us once, to the Brethren of the Twelve, "Brethren, we need to meditate more. We're so busy doing little things. We need to meditate more." I believe, my brethren [and sisters], that we need to (*Teachings of Gordon B. Hinckley*, 334–35).

Just as we hear the voice of the Lord and learn of Him through studying the scriptures, listening to living prophets, and worshipping in the Lord's house, so too can we be strengthened and sustained by meditation. For me, that means a drive by myself in the car where I can think aloud. For others it might be a peaceful walk in nature, some time alone in their room, or prayerful moments in the celestial room. Whatever the specific means, we all need to affirmatively respond to the Good Shepherd's invitation to spiritually "lie down in green pastures" and walk "beside the still waters" so He can restore our souls (see Psalm 23). We all need that kind of restoration work. We all need to focus more clearly. Meditating is focusing. As we focus on Christ by earnestly striving to learn of Him and listen to Him, we will find strength beyond our own.

Learn of me, and listen to my words; walk in the meekness of my Spirit, and you shall have peace in me.

—D&C 19:23

6

Trust in Him

Elijah, my eighteen-month-old grandson, is scared to death of the vacuum cleaner. Not only does he freak out if someone is vacuuming in the room, he also recoils in terror if he sees the inanimate "monster" silently standing in a corner or closet. If he unexpectedly happens to come upon the machine, he shudders with terror and backs away as if it were a rattlesnake. (In fact, he probably would be less afraid of the snake, but Grandpa would have a heart attack.) We don't know why Eli seems to have "vacuum-cleaner phobia," but it is rather amusing to watch him face his greatest fear. We just pray that he doesn't grow up to have issues with vacuums and need therapy before he'll clean his room.

What has been both interesting and inspiring is to see how Elijah's fear fades and courage increases when he is holding my hand. "Out of the mouth of babes" is a familiar saying often used to illustrate how children say something profound or instructional without even knowing what they are saying. Likewise, some lessons are learned "out of the actions of babes"—through things they do when they don't even know we are watching. Such is the case for me as I have observed my grandson. If I hold him in my arms, he will help me vacuum the carpet. If I hold his hand he will even touch the "monster" vacuum. On his own, he is fearful. But with me holding him, he is brave. His trust is stronger than his terror. There is a great lesson in that.

In a similar manner, Eli doesn't do stairs well. His parents have rightfully instilled in him a little fear about going up or down stairs on his own. When the other children go down the stairs to play in Grandma's "play room," Eli wants to join them, but is reluctant. He can't walk down the stairs and he hasn't quite learned (or doesn't want) to crawl down on his belly or scoot down on his behind. When I take him by the hand, however, he has no fear of stairs. He knows that Grandpa won't let him fall. At first, hand-in-hand with me, he would very cautiously take one slow step after another until we made it down all the stairs. Now, however, he takes me by the hand and steps, even jumps, down each stair without any fear or hesitation. In fact, his confidence far exceeds his ability—but only when he has my hand. He has unconditional trust in me. He knows that I love him so much that I won't let go of him.

As I have watched Eli, I have discovered that I am a lot like him. No, I am not afraid of the vacuum cleaner (though Wendy may think I am). I can do stairs on my own quite well (though I may not be as quick in the step as I used to be). I am like my grandson in that I have "monsters" that cause me a degree of fear and trepidation. They are not tangible things, but just as real and debilitating to me as the vacuum cleaner is to Eli. They are emotional monsters like worrying so much about what others think, lack of self-confidence, and perfectionism with its ever-present siblings: self-disappointment, self-deprecation, and discouragement. Perhaps you have similar monsters that you likewise fear. I have come to realize that most of our fears are as irrational and without merit as my grandson's vacuum-cleaner phobia.

In addition to monsters in the closet, we all have mountains to climb that seem as daunting and overwhelming as going down stairs is to a not-so-sure-footed toddler. Our mountain may be responsibilities that require more ability than we feel we have. It may be a task that will require more faith and dedication than anything we have ever faced before. It may be a relationship that seems irreparable. We may feel like we are climbing Mt. Everest in tennis shoes, a light jacket, and without extra oxygen. I have felt that way many times in my own life.

As a grandfather, I delight in helping Eli overcome his fears. There is indescribable joy in having him take my hand to help him down the stairs—knowing that he trusts me so much. I love to hold him and comfort him when he is afraid. I am convinced that the Lord feels the same way about us. He delights in helping us. He loves to hold us and calm our fears. He is pleased when we take His hand. He wants us to trust Him completely. Yet all too often, I, like an unsteady toddler, cower and cry at the top of the stairs, unwilling to take His hand or accept His help—unwilling to lay down my pride, my "pseudo-self-reliance," and rely "wholly upon the merits of him who is mighty to save" (2 Nephi 31:19). Elder Jeffrey R. Holland poignantly observed: "I am convinced that none of us can appreciate how deeply it wounds the loving heart of the Savior of the world when he finds that his people do not feel confident in his care or secure in his hands" ("Come unto Me," *Ensign,* April 1998, 19).

"Trust in the Lord with all thine heart; and lean not unto thine own understanding" (Proverbs 3:5). We have all probably read, heard, and taught this familiar passage many, many times. Of course, we say that we believe it. But do we really? It is easy to say that we believe it, but it is harder than you think to really believe it. From personal experience, I know that it is easier to quote that passage than to live it. The phrase "with all thine heart" implies a total trust, a complete surrender to His will. That kind of trust—the antithesis of leaning on one's own understanding and strength—is difficult for the natural man. It sure is for me! I think that is why the Lord sometimes strips away the security blankets that we cling to—whether they be temporal, emotional, or spiritual—so that we will cling to Him instead. As painful as such experiences are, they enable us to "walk the walk," not just "talk the talk," when it comes to trusting in the Lord and being willing to put our hand in His, figuratively speaking.

Author and Christian apologist C. S. Lewis experienced this himself in a very personal and profound way. He had become famous writing and speaking about Christ's saving power and the necessity of total trust in Him. Yet when his wife died of cancer, Lewis was forced to examine whether his deepest convictions matched his eloquent words. "You never know how much you really believe something," Lewis wrote, "until its truth or falsehood becomes a matter of life and death to you."

> It is easy to say you believe a rope to be strong and sound as long as you are merely using it to cord a box. But suppose you had to hang by that rope over a precipice. Wouldn't you then first discover how much you really trusted it? . . . Only a real risk tests the reality of belief. . . . Nothing less will shake a man—or at any rate a man like me—out of his merely verbal thinking and his merely notional beliefs. He has to be knocked silly before he comes to his senses (*A Grief Observed*, 25, 43).

For me, being "knocked silly" was an emotional breakdown—being forced to my knees, stripped of confidence in myself and my own abilities. To use a boxing metaphor, I was "punched out"—having thrown all the punches I could, I was left with nothing "in the tank," no reservoir of strength on which to fall back. There was only one thing that could be done—throw in the towel. In a boxing match, "throwing in the towel" from a fighter's corner indicates that he is conceding the match—or, to use a term from my childhood, "saying uncle." It is done to prevent further injury to the boxer. The phrase now is used in arenas of life much different than a boxing ring and always means defeat, surrender, giving up.

For me, however, "throwing in the towel"—if it means surrendering to the Savior with total trust—is victory. Only then can we come off conqueror of our respective monsters and mountains. Trusting in the Lord requires us to lay aside the natural man's desire for complete control over his own life and be willing to let the Savior take control. That can be difficult and frightening. For me, giving up control seemed like weakness. In reality, trusting in the Lord is strength. When I focused on Christ by really trusting in Him—His power, His promises, and His love—I found greater capacity, confidence, and charity.

Trust in His Power

When we are discouraged and despondent, when we feel helpless and hopeless, when we have neither the strength nor the will to go on, God can lift us up, empower us, and give guidance to our lives. Although we may feel otherwise at times, we are never left without power to overcome whatever challenges we face, because we always have access to His power—His infinite and awesome power. We know that in our heads. I doubt any of us would deny God's omnipotence. The scriptures are replete with examples of God's power—His power to create all things in heaven and earth, His power over nature, His power over sickness and death, His power over enemies and evil.

Unfortunately, however, when we are down in the dumps or in the depths of despair, we tend to dismiss God's power to save—at least to save us at that moment. We may not say it out loud, but we may think, "Yes, Christ has power to raise Lazarus from the dead, but He can't (or He won't) raise me from my difficulties." Maybe we feel that we brought our problems on ourselves. Maybe we feel that our faith is weak. Maybe we are not as spiritual as we would like. Maybe we feel that we are unworthy of the Lord's attention. Maybe this or maybe that. Maybes don't matter. Trusting in Christ's power is what matters. Faith in Him and being willing to accept the saving power that He extends to us is what is needed at that moment.

Can you imagine being stranded in a terrible blizzard on an isolated road and your car won't start? There you are stuck in a howling snowstorm in subzero temperatures with a dead battery—no heat, no lights, no cell phone, no food, no water, and no hope of getting home. Freezing to death looks like a very real possibility. At the very moment when prospects of rescue seem bleakest, a tow truck pulls up. He has every conceivable tool necessary to make any repair. He has the most powerful battery charger known to man—it never fails to jump a dead battery. In addition, he has brought hot chocolate and warm blankets. Would you say to him, "No, I can't accept your help. I think I inadvertently left the headlights on, so I need to stand out here in the storm to punish myself." Or would you say, "I can fix it myself." Or how about this— "I just don't think your battery charger will work on my car." Or "Your tow chain isn't strong enough." Or "I won't accept your help because you might scratch my car." Or "I don't like hot chocolate."

How ridiculous! We would be so grateful for the lifesaving service. We would gladly place our trust in the tow truck operator and his super duper battery charger. In fact, we would pay almost any price for such roadside assistance. Yet we are sometimes far less willing to trust in the Lord and accept His rescuing power. He can, He will, and He does strengthen us when we find ourselves spiritually or emotionally with a dead battery.

One of my favorite stories in the Old Testament that illustrates God's protective and preserving power is the account of the prophet Elisha and the Syrian armies. The kingdom of Israel had been invaded from the north by the Syrians. Under the inspiration of God, Elisha warned the Israelite king about the invasion and counseled him on how to wage the war against the Syrians. When the Syrian king became aware that Elisha was counseling the king of Israel regarding the positions and strategies of the Syrian army, he sent horses and chariots and numerous soldiers to surround the city and capture Elisha.

"And when the servant of the man of God was risen early, and gone forth, behold, an host compassed the city both with horses and chariots. And his servant said unto him, Alas, my master! how shall we do?" (2 Kings 6:15). In our modern vernacular, the servant is really asking Elisha, "How are we going to get out of this mess? We are totally surrounded!"

I am sure that Elisha's unexpected response led this young servant boy to think either the prophet was totally crazy or hadn't quite awakened and shaken out the cobwebs. Elisha comforted the boy, "Fear not: for they that be with us are more than they that be with them" (2 Kings 6:16).

How could that be? As the servant looked around them, all he could see was hundreds of Syrian soldiers and their horses and chariots. How could anybody in their right mind see that situation and say, "They that be with us are more than they that be with them"? The situation seemed completely hopeless to the young man as he surveyed the odds—one young boy and an aged man against an entire army! It didn't look good.

Elisha must have seen the fear and confusion in the boy's eyes. "And Elisha prayed, and said, Lord, I pray thee, open his eyes, that he may see. And the Lord opened the eyes of the young man; and he saw: and, behold, the mountain was full of horses and chariots of fire round about Elisha" (2 Kings 6:17).

I have shared that story many times and in many settings. I have taught how God's power is always infinitely greater than any power of man or devil. Yet, on one occasion, when I felt particularly beaten down emotionally and struggling with what seemed like an insurmountable obstacle with regards to a problem in our family, Wendy reminded me of this story. She reminded me how often I had used it in talks and lessons. "Don't you believe it?" she asked. When I emphatically declared my belief in God's power, she said, "Then start acting like the power of God really is greater than any challenge we face."

God's power is always there and always available. It is my willingness to trust in that power that wavers from time to time. It is in those moments that I, like Elisha's servant, need to have my spiritual eyes opened. And when they are, I see the power of God and remember how it has been manifest at other times in my life. When my eyes are spiritually open, I recognize that I am not alone or forsaken—the powers of God that are with me are far, far greater than the powers of evil and of the world that are against me.

As I *focus on Christ,* my trust in His power increases. I am convinced that one of the reasons the scriptures are so full of examples and teachings of God's majestic power is to drive the point home to each of us personally that nothing is "too hard for the Lord" (Genesis 18:14). David knew that God was more powerful than Goliath (see 1 Samuel 17). Elijah dramatically demonstrated with consuming fire that Jehovah's power is greater than Baal (see 1 Kings 18). Daniel knew personally that God's power to protect and preserve His people surpassed the devouring power of lions (see Daniel 6). Likewise, Shadrach, Meshach, and Abednego could testify that fiery furnaces can't hold a candle, literally and symbolically, to the glory and power of the Son of Man (see Daniel 3). With just the touch of Jesus' hand, a man blind since birth saw the power of God (see John 9). Jairus witnessed Christ's power to restore life (see Mark 5:35–43). Witnessing the Savior's sea-stilling power, the disciples wondered aloud, "What manner of man is this, that even the winds and the sea obey him!" (see Matthew 8:23–27). Laman and Lemuel experienced with shocking clarity the power of God (see 1 Nephi 17:45–55). The sick, afflicted, lame, and blind at the Nephite temple in Bountiful could teach us something about the power of

Christ's compassion and mercy, and the others could testify of the power of the very words of the risen Lord (see 3 Nephi 17). The scriptural witnesses of the Lord's power are far too numerous to list here.

Evidences of God's power are all around us. Each of us is a witness to that power in our own unique ways. "Can ye dispute the power of God?" (Mosiah 27:15). As I liken the scriptures to myself, I cannot help but be buoyed up as I recognize the power that is available to me for the asking and accepting. In a very personal way, Nephi's "pep talk" to Laman and Lemuel when they doubted their ability to procure the brass plates from Laban is as important to me today it was for them as they cowered in the shadows of Jerusalem's walls.

> And it came to pass that I spake unto my brethren, saying: Let us go up again unto Jerusalem, and let us be faithful in keeping the commandments of the Lord; for behold *he is mightier than all the earth, then why not mightier than Laban and his fifty, yea, or even than his tens of thousands?*
>
> *Therefore let us go up; let us be strong like unto Moses;* for he truly spake unto the waters of the Red Sea and they divided hither and thither, and our fathers came through, out of captivity, on dry ground, and the armies of Pharaoh did follow and were drowned in the waters of the Red Sea.
>
> *Now behold ye know that this is true;* and ye also know that an angel hath spoken unto you; *wherefore can ye doubt? Let us go up; the Lord is able to deliver us, even as our fathers,* and to destroy Laban, even as the Egyptians (1 Nephi 4:1–3; emphasis added).

Trust in His Promises

When I was a child it was not uncommon to "bind" a promise with the words, "Cross my heart and hope to die; stick a thousand pins in my eye." Those words meant that you could not break your word or you would surely have a thousand pins poking you in the eye. Now, I am quite sure that I have never seen anyone with a thousand pins sticking out of their eye. I am equally confident that neither I nor any of my childhood friends kept all of our promises that faithfully and fully. There was always the loophole—the escape clause if you will—of crossing your fingers or toes. Lucky for that, or else I (and everyone else I know) would be blind!

Unfortunately, there are even adults who make promises—whether by their word or through legal contracts, and even with sacred covenants—and yet fail to honor those promises. Probably every person who has ever lived, save One, has fallen short at some time or another in fully honoring a promise given to God or fellowman. Fortunately for us, God is always faithful to His promises. He never "crosses his fingers," says He didn't really mean it, forgets what He said, or falls short in fulfilling what He promised—to the most exacting detail. "Who am I, saith the Lord, that have promised and have not fulfilled?" (D&C 58:31).

Since my birth, every day of my life—whether it has been a good day or bad—has been followed by another day. Even though some sunrises have been less noticeable or spectacular than others and even though I don't remember every one, the sun has never failed to come up, bringing a new day in its rays. It has never failed me. As a result, I have confidence that the sun will again rise tomorrow and the day after and the day after that. My trust in that natural phenomenon is absolute—for I have no reason whatsoever not to trust. As Annie in the Broadway musical sings with complete assurance, we can safely bet our very last dollar that "The sun'll come out tomorrow."

As trustworthy as the sun is, our Father in Heaven and His beloved Son are infinitely more so. Someday even the sun will fail and fade away, but the Lord will never fail us. His promises are sure. There is nothing more reliable. While some may say, "There are no guarantees in life," we know there are. God's promises are guaranteed. We have His word on it!

> Know therefore that the Lord thy God, he is God, the faithful God, which keepeth covenant and mercy with them that love him and keep his commandments to a thousand generations (Deuteronomy 7:9).

> He will swallow up death in victory; and the Lord God will wipe away tears from off all faces; and the rebuke of his people shall he take away from off all the earth: for the Lord hath spoken it (Isaiah 25:8).

> He shall feed his flock like a shepherd: he shall gather the lambs with his arm, and carry them in his bosom, and shall gently lead those that are with young. . . .
> But they that wait upon the Lord shall renew their strength; they shall mount up with wings as eagles; they shall run, and not be weary; and they shall walk, and not faint (Isaiah 40:11, 31).

> Fear thou not; for I am with thee: be not dismayed; for I am thy God: I will strengthen thee; yea, I will help thee; yea, I will uphold thee with the right hand of my righteousness (Isaiah 41:10).

> Fear not: for I have redeemed thee, I have called thee by thy name; thou art mine. . . .
> I am the Lord, your Holy One, the creator of Israel, your King. . . . I, even I, am he that blotteth out thy transgressions

for mine own sake, and will not remember thy sins (Isaiah 43:1, 15, 25).

The Lord is good, a strong hold in the day of trouble; and he knoweth them that trust in him (Nahum 1:7).

Fear thou not: . . . Let not thine hands be slack.

The Lord thy God in the midst of thee is mighty; he will save, he will rejoice over thee with joy; he will rest in his love, he will joy over thee with singing.

I will gather them that are sorrowful. . . . I will undo all that afflict thee: and I will save her that halteth, and gather her that was driven out. . . . I will make you a name and a praise among all people of the earth, when I turn back your captivity before your eyes, saith the Lord (Zephaniah 3:16–20).

I will not leave you comfortless: I will come to you. . . .

Peace I leave with you, my peace I give unto you: not as the world giveth, give I unto you. Let not your heart be troubled, neither let it be afraid (John 14:18, 27).

Ye shall weep and lament, but the world shall rejoice: and ye shall be sorrowful, but your sorrow shall be turned into joy (John 16:20).

Whosoever shall put their trust in God shall be supported in their trials, and their troubles, and their afflictions, and shall be lifted up at the last day (Alma 36:3).

Therefore, fear not, little flock; do good; let earth and hell combine against you, for if ye are built upon my rock, they cannot prevail (D&C 6:34).

I will be merciful unto your weakness. Therefore, be ye strong from henceforth; fear not, for the kingdom is yours (D&C 38:14–15).

Wherefore, be of good cheer, and do not fear, for I the Lord am with you, and will stand by you (D&C 68:6).

Verily, thus saith the Lord unto you—there is no weapon that is formed against you shall prosper. And if any man lift his voice against you he shall be confounded in mine own due time (D&C 71:9–10).

And ye cannot bear all things now; nevertheless, be of good cheer, for I will lead you along. The kingdom is yours and the blessings thereof are yours, and the riches of eternity are yours (D&C 78:18).

I will go before your face. I will be on your right hand and on your left, and my Spirit shall be in your hearts, and mine angels round about you, to bear you up (D&C 84:88).

These are but a few of the myriad promises the Lord has made to us. What strength can be obtained from trusting in them! I have learned from my own experience the very real power these scriptures possess. If we really believe them—take the Lord at His word and trust His promises—we will see that there is no problem or pain that will not be swallowed up by the power and mercy of Christ.

Beyond the scriptures, we have personal promises from the Lord, such as patriarchal blessings, priesthood blessings, inspired promises from the Lord's servants, and promises that come to us by the still, small voice of the Spirit. I have been the beneficiary of such personal promises. So have you. Yet my problem is that I don't always remember them, refer to them, and put my absolute trust in them. When I do, however, there is always a renewed infusion of strength, power, and focus.

One particular, personal promise had special meaning to me as I struggled with the emotional and spiritual challenges that brought me to my knees as a mission president. It was a promise—an apostolic blessing—given to mission presidents and their wives by President Boyd K. Packer. Wendy and I were so inspired by his words that we printed them on a poster board and taped it to the mirror in the master bedroom of the mission home. We read those words each day. When times were most difficult and trying, we would encourage each other to "trust in the promise!"

You will be attended constantly by angels who will speak to you by the power of the Holy Ghost. . . . The ministering of those beyond the veil over this work is constant. The pattern of revelation is constant. The concern of them beyond the veil for us is incessant. And you will be the beneficiaries of a guidance and watch care that will see you move out into the challenging world that you have and be able to not only accomplish that which you are called to do, but you will be able to rejoice in it notwithstanding the challenges. And you will come with a certainty and a testimony and spiritual growth that you have not dreamed of. . . .

[I bless you that] you will be watched over, that the Spirit of the Lord will be with you, that angels will attend you. And that you will be blessed in your homes, your families, your children, and their children. And blessings that are of deep concern to you, you will find them unfolding, and if you will be patient, you will find that as you look after the Lord's children, He'll be looking after yours (President Boyd K. Packer, New Mission Presidents Seminar, Missionary Training Center, June 1998).

Only when I finally came to believe those words and trust in the Lord's other remarkable promises did I begin to see light at the end of the tunnel. In that light, I began to see and appreciate their fulfillment in my life, in my family, and in my ministry. Although President Packer's apostolic blessing was directed to new mission presidents and their wives, his promises are encompassed, even surpassed, by those given us by the Lord Himself. The Savior's promises are to all— regardless of our calling or circumstance. He does not lie. He will not go back on His word. Our need is but to trust in Him, believe His promises, and not lose sight of them in times of trial.

"No matter how serious the trial, how deep the distress, how great the affliction, He will never desert us," President George Q. Cannon taught. "He never has, and He never will. He cannot do it."

It is not His character [to do so]. He is an unchangeable being; the same yesterday, the same today, and He will be the same throughout the eternal ages to come. We have found that God. We have made Him our friend, by obeying His gospel; and He will stand by us. We may pass through the fiery furnace; we may pass through deep waters; but we shall not be consumed nor overwhelmed. We shall emerge from all these trials and difficulties the better and purer for them, if we will only trust in our God and keep His commandments (In *Collected Discourses*, 2:185).

Trust in His Love

There have been times when I've felt much like Nephi when the angel asked him concerning the meaning of the "condescension" of God (see 1 Nephi 11). "I do not know the meaning of all things," he stated. I could relate to that. I don't know exactly what *conditional, perfect, unconditional,* or *divine* fully mean any more than Nephi knew everything there was to know about condescension. But like Nephi, "I know that he loveth his children" (1 Nephi 11:17), and that's what matters most. I know that God loves me, because I am His child. He is my heavenly Father. I know that Jesus loves me, for He bought me with His blood. He is my Savior, my Redeemer, my rock, and my salvation. Knowledge of that divine love and those eternal relationships is to me, as Paul declared of hope, "an anchor of the soul, both sure and stedfast" (Hebrews 6:19).

In the *Lectures on Faith,* the Prophet Joseph Smith taught that without a correct idea concerning God's nature and attributes "the faith of every rational being must be imperfect and unproductive" (p. 38). Without abiding trust in God's perfect attributes such as knowledge, justice, mercy, judgment, and truth, "men could not have confidence sufficient to place themselves under his guidance and direction" (p. 52).

One of the attributes of God in which we can have complete confidence is His perfect love for us. The Prophet taught that "with all the other excellencies in his character, without this one to influence them, they could not have such powerful dominion over the minds of men; but when the idea is planted in the mind that [God] is love, who cannot see the just ground that men of every nation, kindred, and tongue, have to exercise faith in God so as to obtain eternal life?" (p. 43).

As I understand it, the more I trust in God's perfect love, the more I will trust in His other attributes, His promises, His laws and commandments. The more I trust in and feel His pure love the greater will be my faith in the Savior of the world and the stronger my desires to follow Him. Divine love—charity, the pure love of Christ—is the great motivator, the great healer, the great peace giver. Love is the greatest catalyst for enduring change.

> I have loved thee with an everlasting love: therefore with lovingkindness have I drawn thee (Jeremiah 31:3).

Who shall separate us from the love of Christ? shall tribulation, or distress, or persecution, or famine, or nakedness, or peril, or sword? . . .

For I am persuaded, that neither death, nor life, nor angels, nor principalities, nor powers, nor things present, nor things to come, nor height, nor depth, nor any other creature, shall be able to separate us from the love of God, which is in Christ Jesus our Lord (Romans 8:35, 38–39).

That Christ may dwell in your hearts by faith; that ye, being rooted and grounded in love, may be able to comprehend with all saints what is the breadth, and length, and depth, and height; and to know the love of Christ, which passeth knowledge, that ye might be filled with all the fulness of God (Ephesians 3:17–19).

But behold, the Lord hath redeemed my soul from hell; I have beheld his glory, and I am encircled about eternally in the arms of his love (2 Nephi 1:15).

He doeth not anything save it be for the benefit of the world; for he loveth the world, even that he layeth down his own life that he may draw all men unto him. Wherefore, he commandeth none that they shall not partake of his salvation (2 Nephi 26:24).

But charity is the pure love of Christ, and it endureth forever; and whoso is found possessed of it at the last day, it shall be well with him (Moroni 7:47).

When I was at an emotional low point in my life, Wendy held me in her arms and urged me to "focus on Christ." Specifically, she urged me to focus on and trust in His perfect love for me. I could not do a lot of things at that moment, but I could feel His love. I knew that no matter who I was, no matter where I was, no matter what my challenges or weaknesses, I was loved with His pure love. Though I may fail and falter, the Savior's love for me will never fail. Because of my simple trust in that eternal fact, I could be confident that I could face any challenge and surmount any difficulty, however long and hard the road. The words and testimony of Elder Jeffrey R. Holland echoed in my soul as I clung to the Savior's perfect love as my emotional and spiritual lifeline:

Life has its share of some fear and some failure. Sometimes things fall short, don't quite measure up. Sometimes in both personal and public life, we are seemingly left without strength to go on. Sometimes people fail us, or economies and circumstances fail us, and life with its hardship and heartache can leave us feeling very alone.

But when such difficult moments come to us, I testify that there is one thing which will never, ever fail us. One thing alone will stand the test of all time, of all tribulation, all trouble, and all transgression. One thing only never faileth—and that is the pure love of Christ.

. . . Only the pure love of Christ will see us through. It is Christ's love which suffereth long and is kind. It is Christ's love which is not puffed up nor easily provoked. Only His pure love enables Him—and us—to bear all things, believe all things, hope all things, and endure all things (see Moro. 7:45).

Oh, love effulgent, love divine!
What debt of gratitude is mine,
That in his off'ring I have part
And hold a place within his heart.

I testify that having loved us who are in the world, Christ loves us to the end. His pure love never fails us. Not now. Not ever. Not ever. Of that divine sustaining vote for all of us, I testify (*Trusting Jesus,* 80–81).

At times in our lives, each of us will be like my grandson—afraid and unsure of ourselves. No doubt, our fear will be of something much different than Eli's "vacuum cleaner monster," but it will be real. We will desperately need a comforting hand to ease that fear and soothe our soul with a comforting "everything will be alright" assurance. At other times, our feelings of inadequacy and lack of confidence will, undoubtedly, involve something more than "doing stairs," but our need for strength and capacity beyond our own will be just as pronounced. How grateful I am that I, like my grandson, can trust in the support and strength of another. Trusting in God—His power, His promises, and His love—is the way we reach out to accept the divine helping hand that steadies and strengthens us.

> *He only is my rock and my salvation: he is my defence; I shall not be moved.*
> *In God is my salvation and my glory: the rock of my strength, and my refuge, is in God.*
> *Trust in him at all times; ye people, pour out your heart before him: God is a refuge for us.*
>
> —Psalm 62:6–8

7

HOLD ON TO HIM

Recently I saw a remarkable news story broadcast on a sports channel on television. It was a story of courage, determination, and endurance. I am a sports fanatic, and such stories of overcoming great odds with incredible determination and focus are always inspiring to me. This particular story that captured my attention was about Claire Markwardt, a high school senior and cross-country runner from Berkshire High School in Ohio. In the weeks before the state championship race, Claire felt pain in her left leg. Thinking it was typical soreness stemming from a muscle strain, there was no thought of not competing in the biggest race of her life. On pace to achieve a personal-best record, Claire heard a crack in her leg with about a quarter of a mile left in the race. About 200 meters later, there was another crack and then a loud pop. Her entire leg gave out and she collapsed on the track. Not knowing what had happened, Claire's teammates encouraged her to get up and finish the race.

"At that point, I knew what had happened. I knew my leg was broken pretty badly," Claire said. "I had come so far. Our team had come so far. All season, we had been working for state, and now we were there. I was almost done, and there was no way I was going to let the team down."

Claire literally crawled the last forty-five feet of the race, finishing only eighteen seconds off her personal best time.

I couldn't believe what I saw. Here was a young woman with a broken fibula and multiple breaks in her tibia, crawling on her hands and knees to the finish line. The pain must have been intense beyond description. Yet her focus on the finish line, her determination to finish the race and not let her teammates down, drew out of her remarkable courage and endurance. It was an inspiration to me and undoubtedly to thousands of others (see "High School Runner Breaks Leg in Meet, Crawls to Finish Anyway," espn.com).

We hear a lot in the Church about enduring to the end, and rightfully so. It is a fundamental principle of the gospel that is clearly and repeatedly taught in the scriptures. For me, however, when I am in an emotionally "beaten and bruised" condition—when I feel so overwhelmed, inadequate, and so far beneath what I want to be and what I think the Lord expects of me—enduring to the end is not a happy or hopeful-sounding gospel principle. Perhaps you have wondered at times, like I have, "How can I endure to the end when I can't even endure this moment?" I believe that my bad attitude about endurance (and that of many others who may feel like giving up when they hear the word) comes from a doctrinal misunderstanding of what the Lord really expects of us. "Buck up," "Grit your teeth," "Put your shoulder to the wheel," "Grin and bear it," "Tough it out," are all phrases that immediately come to mind when I think of endurance. The visual image in my mind is of this courageous young cross-country runner, with a badly broken leg, crawling all alone to the finish line.

Part of my misunderstanding of this doctrine is that I have believed, mostly subconsciously, that enduring to the end is something that must be done all by one's self—what I call "pseudo-self-reliance." Sometimes we fall into the trap of thinking that we must do everything on our own and that it is only those weak in the faith that reach out for help. I do not think that is what the Lord wants me to believe. In fact, I know that He doesn't want me to believe such a notion. I can't imagine the Savior standing over me when I have fallen in the race of life—when I have spiritual or emotional "broken legs," when I am painfully crawling along, or when I am barely hanging on by my fingernails—and scolding me with words such as, "Buck up, little camper," or "You gotta be tough, if you're going to be a disciple." No, I can't imagine that. If that was my image of the Master, I would surely give up. Thank goodness that the scriptures portray a much different view of the Lord—an image of love and compassion, an image of an outstretched hand that will lift us up, strengthen us, and see us through to the finish line. We are not left alone to crawl on our hands and knees. His grace enables our "enduring to the end." Lehi's vision of the tree of life illustrates this doctrine well:

> And I saw numberless concourses of people, many of whom were pressing forward, that they might obtain the path which led unto the tree by which I stood.
>
> And it came to pass that they did come forth, and commence in the path which led to the tree.
>
> And it came to pass that there arose a mist of darkness; yea, even an exceedingly great mist of darkness, insomuch that they who had commenced in the path did lose their way, that they wandered off and were lost.
>
> And it came to pass that I beheld others pressing forward, and they came forth and caught hold of the end of the rod of iron; and they did press forward through the mist of darkness,

clinging to the rod of iron, even until they did come forth and partake of the fruit of the tree.

And after they had partaken of the fruit of the tree they did cast their eyes about as if they were ashamed.

And I also cast my eyes round about, and beheld, on the other side of the river of water, a great and spacious building; and it stood as it were in the air, high above the earth.

And it was filled with people, both old and young, both male and female; and their manner of dress was exceedingly fine; and they were in the attitude of mocking and pointing their fingers towards those who had come at and were partaking of the fruit.

And after they had tasted of the fruit they were ashamed, because of those that were scoffing at them; and they fell away into forbidden paths and were lost.

And now I, Nephi, do not speak all of the words of my father.

But, to be short in writing, behold, he saw other multitudes pressing forward; and they came and caught hold of the end of the rod of iron; and they did press their way forward, continually holding fast to the rod of iron, until they came forth and fell down and partook of the fruit of the tree (1 Nephi 8:21–30).

Lehi saw the faithful "pressing forward" to the tree of life, secured by "continually holding fast to the rod of iron." Nephi teaches us that the iron rod is the word of God (see 1 Nephi 15:23–24). There are several passages in the Bible where John the Beloved identifies Christ Himself as the Word of God (see John 1:1, 14; JST, John 1:16; Revelation 19:11–16). In this light, Lehi and Nephi are teaching us that Christ is both the means—the rod of iron—and the end—the tree of life. What a difference it should make to us to know that amidst all of the "mists of darkness" in the world and the scoffing and mockings from the "great and spacious building" we are not left to find our way alone! The Savior—the Word of God—is not merely pointing directions and shouting encouragement from the shade of the tree of life. As the iron rod, Jesus provides us the only way to our desired end and also our protection against the mists of darkness and the taunts from the great and spacious building. "Whoso would hearken unto the word of God, and would hold fast unto it," Nephi declares, "they would never perish; neither could the temptations and the fiery darts of the adversary overpower them unto blindness, to lead them away to destruction" (1 Nephi 15:24).

Do you notice that no one makes it to the tree of life without taking hold of the iron rod? It is not just a matter of "pressing forward." Notice that not one of the "numberless concourses of people" seen by Lehi and Nephi came and partook of the fruit of the tree without tightly holding to the rod of iron. Not one made it on his own—no matter how hard he tried, no matter how determined he was, no matter how good his sense of direction. On the other hand, every one that let go of the rod was lost—either lost in the mists of darkness, drowned in the depths of the filthy river, or "lost" in a different way in the great and spacious building.

There have been many times in my life when I have tried to partake of the fruit—that "most sweet" fruit that is "desirable to make one happy" and that fills the soul "with exceedingly great joy" (1 Nephi 8:10–12) by just "pressing forward" on my own. I don't think I was conscious of the fact that I was doing it, but it was like I was just gritting my teeth and pushing forward against the "mists of darkness" and the "fiery darts of the adversary." At times, when my path paralleled the rod of iron, I probably made good progress. At other times, however, I got lost or my strength abandoned me, and I was essentially left crawling on my hands and knees.

That was the condition in which I found myself while serving as a mission president. I could not just "buck up," "tough it out," or "press forward." I needed a helping hand—the outstretched hand of the Lord. Now when I think of the iron rod, I don't just think of a narrow path and an iron-rod railing. I think of Him with outstretched hand and arms of mercy wide open. Even if I am battered, bruised, broken down, and crawling, as it were, on hands and knees, I just need to grab hold of that hand—and never let go. With my hand in His, only then does my "pressing forward" lead me to the tree. I don't have to find my own way to the tree (in fact, I can't). I just need to find my way to the rod, then reach up, take hold, and hang on. Only then is my pressing forward—whether fast or slow, big strides or baby steps—with "a steadfastness in Christ" and a "perfect brightness of hope" going to enable me to endure to the end (see 2 Nephi 31:20). To endure to the end is not just to keep going. It is taking hold of His rescuing hand, holding on tight, following where He guides us, and never, never letting go.

Not many months before our mission ended, the mother of one of our missionaries passed away. She had been diagnosed with a serious illness, but the doctors and family were hopeful of, if not a full recovery, at least many years of life. Unfortunately, her condition deteriorated much more quickly than was expected. Her death was both sudden and shocking—especially to her son serving in our mission. I had the dreaded task of informing him. I prayed for guidance. I wanted to say just the right thing so that this elder would be comforted in his grief and strengthened in his service.

I felt inspired to take the elder and his companion to the Nauvoo Temple, where I broke the news as we sat in a sealing room. It was a tender and sacred moment. We were alone in the room, but not alone. The veil was indeed thin. My heart was drawn out in love and compassion for this missionary to a remarkable extent—not because of my natural emotions, but as a result of a spiritual gift from the Divine. I felt both humbled and honored to share in this sacred moment and experience those sacred feelings.

In the months that followed, I was inspired by how this young man dealt with his loss and heartache. Not for a moment had he considered cutting his mission short and going home. Not for a moment did his pace slacken or did his work suffer. In fact, he worked harder and, in many ways, was even more effective as a missionary. I worried that he was in denial, suppressing his true feelings. There was a concern that he hadn't dealt with his grief and that he would eventually crash and burn. Yet I didn't see evidence of any of that. He bore this challenge with incredible strength and grace. How was he able to do it?

Not long ago, Sister Top and I attended the sacrament meeting where this remarkable young man reported his mission. We saw a stark contrast between this spiritually mature, confident, powerful missionary and the fearful, struggling nineteen-year-old who had come to our mission two years earlier. The Spirit of the Lord was upon him. There was no doubt about that. As he spoke of his mother's death and how he dealt with it, he made a simple observation that powerfully affected me. "I held on to the iron rod," he declared, "even when I couldn't see the tree of life." That is faith. That is "press[ing] forward with a steadfastness in Christ." That is enduring.

When I was a Boy Scout, I took a swimming and lifesaving class. In addition to learning the various swimming strokes, we also practiced rescue techniques. Our instructor warned us of the danger in approaching a drowning person—even when he knows you are trying to rescue him. Often the panic that sets in causes him to thrash about and grab in such a way that makes lifesaving efforts impossible and may actually lead to both parties being drowned. A drowning person desperately desires to be saved, but in the panic doesn't know how. The lifesaver has to help the victim "let go, look up, and hold on"—let go of your own panicky efforts, look up in trust to the rescuer, take hold of his hand, and allow him to carry you to safety.

Spiritually, it works much the same way. We swim as hard and as far as we can—never able to reach the shore solely through our own efforts. When that reality sets in, we may panic, grab at anything and everything, thrash about until our strength is gone, and then cry out in agony. "The time when there is nothing at all in your soul except for a cry for help may be just the time when God can't give it," C. S. Lewis wrote. "You are like the drowning man who can't be helped because he clutches and grabs. Perhaps your own reiterated cries deafen you to the voice you hoped to hear" (*A Grief Observed*, 53–54).

At that point there are really only two choices—drown or take hold of the rescuing hand of the Lord. If I choose to take the Savior's hand and allow Him to rescue me—"be still" and let go of my own futile efforts to be in control—then will I find greater strength to hold on. Cradled in the saving and secure grasp of the Master, I find that I can swim along with less effort and worry—knowing that He will buoy me up and strengthen me. My efforts are given renewed power because I realize He will not let go of me. I will only "drown" if I let go of Him.

Last summer was one of the hottest on record. My grandchildren didn't mind, however. They loved running through the sprinklers in our backyard and having water fights with Grandma. What started with squirt guns soon progressed to buckets and hoses. I don't know how you determine who the winner is when all the participants in the water fight are totally soaked. But my five-year-old grandson, Caleb, proudly proclaimed himself the winner. "I am really good at this," he exulted. When I asked him why he was so good, I expected some explanation of water-fight strategy. Instead, he simply declared, "I always win, because I never give up!"

So it is spiritually. We will win the prize—we will partake of the fruit of the tree of life—if we don't give up. We will be made perfect and enjoy eternal life if we hold on to the Savior and don't let go. That is His promise and only we ourselves, by failing to take His outstretched hand, can prevent that from becoming reality. As C. S. Lewis wrote:

> You must realise from the outset that the goal towards which He is beginning to guide you is absolute perfection; *and no power in the whole universe, except you yourself, can prevent Him from taking you to that goal. . . .*
>
> The command *Be ye perfect* is not idealistic gas. Nor is it a command to do the impossible. He is going to make us into creatures that can obey that command. He said (in the Bible) that we were "gods" and He is going to make good His words. *If we let Him—for we can prevent Him, if we choose*—He will make the feeblest and filthiest of us into a god or goddess, a dazzling, radiant, immortal creature, pulsating all through with such energy and joy and wisdom and love as we cannot now imagine, a bright stainless mirror which reflects back to God perfectly . . . His own boundless power and delight and goodness. The process will be long and in parts very painful, but that is what we are in for. Nothing less (*Mere Christianity*, 203, 205–6; emphasis added).

As I strive to press forward with "a steadfastness in Christ" I hold on to Him by doing the best I can. Even when I can't see the tree of life for the mists of darkness and when it feels like I am climbing Mt. Everest, I can do my best. At times, my best hasn't been as great as at other times. Sometimes my best is doing much and sometimes it is doing only little. Certainly, my best may not be as good as your best. And though our bests may vary, we don't compete or compare. "Only the Lord can compare crosses," Elder Neal A. Maxwell observed, "but all crosses are easier to carry when we keep moving" (*The Neal A. Maxwell Quotebook,* 5).

Keeping moving—whether I am moving quickly or slowly, whether I untiringly push forward or have to stop occasionally to "lean upon my sword and rest a little" (see Ether 15:30)—and doing my best is all I've got to give, and sometimes that isn't much. "Those who do right, and seek the glory of the Father in heaven," President Brigham Young taught, "whether they can do little or much, if they do the very best they know how, they are perfect. . . . When we are doing as well as we know in the sphere, and station which we occupy here we are justified. . . . We are as justified as the angels who are before the throne of God" (in *Deseret News Weekly,* August 31, 1854, 37).

As someone once said, "I did what I knew and when I knew better, I did better." That is doing our best and that is the "all we can do" which opens the door for His difference-making, heart-healing, and strength-giving grace (see 2 Nephi 25:23). I can't do everything, but I can keep trusting, holding on to the Savior, repenting of my sins, and striving to do what's right. Even if I have to crawl on my hands and knees to the finish line, He'll help me. I know that with all my heart. I have been carried when I was spiritually broken. By holding on to Him, I have come to understand that five-year-old Caleb has it right—we will always win, if we don't give up.

For I the Lord thy God will hold thy right hand, saying unto thee, Fear not; I will help thee.

—Isaiah 41:13

8

STRENGTHENED BY THE HAND OF THE LORD

WHEN I AM WEAK, THEN AM I strong," the Apostle Paul wrote the Corinthian Saints. How can that be? In contrast to Paul's noble sentiments, I have been known to say, "When I am weak, then am I weak. Woe is me." I must admit that, unlike Paul, I don't "take pleasure in infirmities, in reproaches, in necessities, . . . in distresses" (2 Corinthians 12:10). Let's face it, I am a wimp! I admit it. I don't do pain well. It hurts! Depression depresses me. Discouragement discourages me. Sniffles and a sore throat cause me to feel that I am at death's door. I don't like to suffer. In fact, I am insufferable in suffering! I guess that is why I appreciate the sentiments of this humorous poem, entitled "Smile, Darned You, Smile."

> If you can smile when things go wrong,
> And say it doesn't matter,
> If you can laugh off cares and woe,
> And troubles make you fatter,
> If you can keep a cheerful face
> When all around are blue,

> Then have your head examined, bud,
> There's something wrong with you.
> For one thing I've arrived at:
> There are no ands and buts,
> A guy that's grinning all the time
> Must be completely nuts.
>
> —Quoted by Boyd K. Packer in
> *"Let Not Your Heart Be Troubled,"* 247

I don't think Paul was "completely nuts," nor do I think he was just a "put on a happy face" optimist when he talked about glorying in his infirmities. The scriptures provide us with a record of all the hardships and persecutions associated with his ministry (see 2 Corinthians 11:23–33). In addition, this powerful missionary-apostle gave us a glimpse into how he dealt with tribulation and adversity: "And lest I should be exalted above measure through the abundance of the revelations," he wrote, "there was given to me a thorn in the flesh, the messenger of Satan to buffet me" (2 Corinthians 12:7).

We don't know what that "thorn in the flesh" was. Scholars have speculated for centuries. What we do know is that it was a personal trial of such a nature that Paul was "forced to his knees" on at least three occasions to plead with the Lord "that it might depart from me" (2 Corinthians 12:8). Whether that "thorn in the flesh" was physical, emotional, spiritual, or a combination of all of them, it must have been a heavy burden to bear.

No doubt Paul thought he would be better able to serve the Lord if he wasn't so afflicted. But the Lord knew better! Paul had unique qualifications. He had received a first-rate education and rabbinical training. He was extraordinarily talented, intelligent, and eloquent. He knew the scriptures, was spiritual, and had been blessed with powerful revelations. Yet, despite all of these advantages, his "thorn in the flesh" is what transformed his ministry—because it "forced" him to rely on the Lord and be strengthened by His outstretched hand.

When Paul was down in the dumps because of his afflictions, when he was once again pleading with God to remove the thorn, the Lord spoke to Paul's soul and said, "My grace is sufficient for thee: for my strength is made perfect in weakness" (2 Corinthians 12:9). It was at that point that Paul understood that because of his weaknesses and afflictions—all of those things that made him feel inadequate, discouraged, overwhelmed—he could come unto the Lord in a way that he probably wouldn't if he had no "thorns in the flesh." In that manner, the Savior sanctified his weaknesses and turned them into strengths by "the power of Christ."

Jesus will do the same for us. We, like Paul, can glory in our infirmities—though not infirmities themselves or suffering merely for suffering's sake—because, if we will allow it, "the power of Christ" rests upon us in our afflictions. When that happens, no matter what our individual "thorns in the flesh" may be, we are strong. That is what Paul means when he says, "when I am weak, then am I strong." Book of Mormon prophets also understood and taught this doctrine. "My grace is sufficient for the meek," the Lord told Moroni.

> And if men come unto me I will show unto them their weakness. I give unto men weakness that they may be humble; and my grace is sufficient for all men that humble themselves before me; for *if they humble themselves before me, and have faith in me, then will I make weak things become strong unto them* (Ether 12:26–27; emphasis added).

"He Will Take upon Him the Pains and Sicknesses of His People"

We have a grandson who was born with a birth defect. The lower part of his left arm and hand did not properly develop in utero. He refers to his short arm and undeveloped hand as his nub. (As you can imagine, *Finding Nemo* is one of his favorite movies.) Although it hasn't slowed him down very much and he certainly doesn't consider himself handicapped, he does notice that he is different than others. He is getting to the age now where he is conscious of the stares and unkind comments about his nub. He recently told his mother that he wanted two hands like all of his friends. His "thorn in the flesh" was starting to become emotionally painful to bear—both for him and for all of us who love him so much and want the best for him. We hurt when he hurts. We feel badly when he feels badly.

In decorating her home for Christmas, our daughter put out the olive wood nativity set she received from us as a Christmas gift when we lived in Israel many years ago. It had taken a few hits through the years and through the many moves it had been through. There were a few chips and dents and a piece broken off here and there. One day, three-year-old Gavin excitedly exclaimed, "Mommy, look! Jesus has a nub just like me!" Part of one of the carved wooden arms of the baby Jesus in the nativity set had been broken off. Who knows when the damage had occurred? It was so small that none of us had even noticed before. Yet Gavin noticed. He was thrilled that Jesus had a nub too. His mother explained to him that Jesus doesn't really have a nub, but that He understands exactly what it is like for Gavin to have one.

In that tender teaching moment, she once again taught him about the resurrection and how Jesus' Atonement ensures that someday Gavin will have a hand like everyone else. That satisfied him. "That's okay, Mommy," Gavin said. "I like my nub. I'll keep it forever."

What had been seen as a handicap—a burden, an embarrassment—was now seen from a much different perspective. Gavin was able to deal with his challenge better because he understood, even as a three-year-old, that Jesus understands what it is like to have a nub and that He will help Gavin throughout life and someday give him a glorified body with an arm and hand that were missing in mortality.

Just as Gavin rejoiced in Jesus having a nub like him, we all long to know that Jesus understands us, relates to us personally, and can succor us in our unique challenges and "thorns in the flesh." We all want to have Jesus a little more like us, so we can trust that He really knows our pains and understands our weaknesses. Thankfully, prophets and apostles have testified that we indeed have a Savior who not only understands the burdens we carry, but carried them Himself long before we bore them. He can strengthen us in our suffering because He suffered all that we have to endure, and more, before we did.

In fact, Jesus knows what it is like to be every one of us. He knows us personally. He knows what we struggle with and what pains afflict us, because He experienced it all when He descended below all things (see D&C 122:8). That painful descent was part of what Elder Neal A. Maxwell called the "awful arithmetic of the Atonement" (see "Willing to Submit," *Ensign*, May 1985, 73). Alma declared:

> And he shall go forth, suffering pains and afflictions and temptations of every kind; and this that the word might be fulfilled which saith he will take upon him the pains and the sicknesses of his people.
>
> And he will take upon him . . . their infirmities, that his bowels may be filled with mercy, according to the flesh, that he may know according to the flesh how to succor his people according to their infirmities (Alma 7:11–12).

Succor is not a word that we use much in our normal, everyday conversations. Yet it is a powerful word that conjures important images of help and aid. The word comes from the Latin *succurrere,* which means literally "to run to help." It implies urgent assistance. Have you ever succored someone—literally run to his assistance? Probably every parent has had the experience of hearing the blood-curdling cry of an injured child. We bolt into action immediately—a nanosecond probably doesn't even pass before we are off to the rescue. There is nothing that prevents us from running to that beloved child.

Do you see the beauty of that imagery as you read Alma's words again? Do you see the Savior bearing your burdens as well as mine, suffering your personal pains and mine, feeling our individual feelings of discouragement, inadequacy, and fear? What an incredible thought—because Jesus is filled with infinite compassion and mercy, because He intimately knows me and you, because He has been literally "touched with the feeling of our infirmities" (Hebrews 4:15)—He "runs to" our assistance! What comfort! What hope! What strength! I have felt His succoring aid.

At the first of this book, I told you that this was a deeply personal story. I have shared with you my struggles with depression, anxiety, inadequacy, self-doubt, and fear. (You may have always suspected that I was a "basket case"; now I have removed all doubt.) While there may be some cathartic value in self-disclosure, I find it difficult—like opening up a vein. Just disclosing my difficulties and sharing my story doesn't necessarily help anyone—myself included. "Opening up a vein" only causes one to bleed to death. What helps is a transfusion. I have been open about my challenges, not merely because I want you to know that you are not alone in bearing "thorns in the flesh," but to help you to know how to take hold of the succoring hand of the Master. In helping you, I continue to help me. I have shared with you lessons I have learned through the years—principles and practices that have helped me to focus on Christ and receive the abundant life-giving and lifesaving transfusion that only He can provide.

As a religious educator, I think often on President Harold B. Lee's counsel to gospel teachers to teach "not so plain that they can just understand, but you must teach the doctrines of the Church so plainly that no one can misunderstand" (*The Teachings of Harold B. Lee*, 459). In telling of my experiences and teaching the principles I have learned, I hope that you will not only understand plainly, but also that you will not misunderstand. To accomplish that, it is necessary that I tell you the "rest of the story."

After I had my breakdown and Wendy held me in her arms and encouraged me to focus on Christ, I was not immediately healed. Although I felt immediate comfort and love, the healing was a learning process, not an event. It is still ongoing. There have been good days and bad days, as there probably always will be. Fortunately, there are more good days than bad. Sometimes I practice the skills I have learned and exercise the faith I have obtained through this experience better than at other times. I have noticed that when the process of healing seems slow, it is easy to get discouraged and feel like giving up—we stop "pressing forward." On the other hand, when we feel great and it seems as if everything is "back to normal" (whatever normal is) there is a temptation to loosen our grip on the iron rod, not focus as intently on the Master as we should, and rely on our own strengths—we fall back into the trap of running faster than we have strength.

That is why the healing process is just that—a process of relearning, reapplying the lessons learned, and becoming refocused and redirected. Good days and bad days are not necessarily successes and failures, respectively. Both the good and the bad, the difficult and the easy, the painful and the comfortable can teach us valuable lessons. If we are learning and improving, each day exercising more faith in the Lord and continually striving to take hold of and hang on tight to His outstretched hand, then we are successful—even though we may not see the growth or the healing. It usually occurs slowly, almost imperceptibly, rather than in one dramatic event.

I was profoundly different at the end of our three-year mission than I was at the first part, but that transformation came slowly—so gradually that the changes weren't readily apparent, even to me. There were still worries and fears, feelings of inadequacy and being overwhelmed. There was still plenty of stress and anxiety. Depression, like alcoholism, is never totally cured. It is ever-present, but dealt with in constructive ways. The outside influences remained the same, but the internal reactions were different.

When a General Authority and his wife toured our mission, near the end of our three-year term of service, he asked, "How are you able to do all this so well?" Wendy and I looked at each other and thought to ourselves, "If he only knew!" He didn't know the struggles and emotional breakdowns at the first of our mission. He only observed how we were doing at that moment. He was looking at our destination, not aware of the journey.

"Drugs," I facetiously responded. "We are able to make it because of the drugs." It wasn't entirely a joke. My doctor had prescribed antidepressant and anti-anxiety medications. I am thankful for the help they provided. They were an important part of my healing process—but not the only, or most important, part.

The General Authority didn't condemn me, judge me, or look down his nose at me. He was very understanding and compassionate. He assured me that it was not that uncommon. In fact, he said we would be surprised at how many suffer similarly. Some of the Lord's most powerful leaders have struggled with depression. Yet with help, both mortal and divine, they had risen to great heights and rendered significant service in the kingdom.

Unfortunately, there is a stigma attached to taking medication or receiving professional help for emotional problems—a stigma that doesn't seem to be attached to other medical conditions and needs. Many are quick to assume that a person who takes medication for an emotional illness either lacks sufficient faith to be healed or has other spiritual problems in his life. Would you think that a diabetic who takes insulin lacks faith? What about a person who takes cholesterol-lowering medication? Is the person who needs blood-pressure regulating drugs a sinner? Of course not! We recognize that medications and treatments, administered under the direction of competent professionals, have their place and do much good. So it is in dealing with emotional challenges. Medication, however, cannot be the only remedy—any more than cholesterol-lowering drugs can cure heart disease without proper diet, exercise, and other ongoing therapies.

One of my missionaries who was struggling with serious emotional challenges that were impeding his work resisted my suggestions that he get professional help, including medication if necessary. "I want to be able to feel the Spirit," he said. He assumed that taking an antidepressant would stifle spirituality and prevent him from receiving necessary direction by the still, small voice.

I was taken aback by his comment. I am not a physician, a pharmacist, or psychologist, but I have had some experience with each of them. For me (and I can only speak for me), receiving professional help opened the door to greater spiritual help. I could not feel the Spirit as I desired when I was in the deep, dark hole of depression. But when proper medical therapy was coupled with spiritual therapy I began to see the "light at the end of the tunnel"—I could feel the Spirit again in my life. I may have felt better emotionally with only medical treatment, but I could not have learned the valuable lessons of life nor could I have gained the unspeakable spiritual strength and power that comes from "relying wholly upon the merits of him who is mighty to save" (2 Nephi 31:19). Focusing on Christ powerfully affected me—

physically, emotionally, and spiritually. My emotional and physical stamina increased, and my spiritual strength and sensitivities intensified. Like getting in shape, it didn't happen suddenly, but over time and with much effort.

A comment from one of the senior office missionaries made me realize I had, indeed, been remarkably changed. "President Top never gets rattled by anything," the senior elder said. "He is unflappable."

Unflappable? I wanted to laugh out loud. That was a word I would never have used to describe myself. At emotional low points, I was anything but unflappable. I was often "flapped." (I don't know if that's a word, but it sounds good.) My emotional and spiritual equilibrium were easily disrupted. I often felt like I was "falling apart at the seams." But over time, as I sought to focus on Christ—as I willingly put my burdens on Him and took His strengthening and guiding hand in mine—my reactions to problems and pressures changed. Instead of fear, there was faith. I had feared because of my own abilities (or lack of them), but when I had to trust in the Lord (because I had nothing left but that), confidence replaced consternation.

When I was relying mostly on myself—focusing on my many weaknesses and lack of confidence and ability—I dreaded the responsibilities, problems, and pressures. When I focused on Christ—though I didn't necessarily love problems and seek them out—I felt a confidence that, as President Gordon B. Hinckley often said, "Things will all work out." Infused with that spiritual confidence, I found greater joy and fulfillment in my service, and my efforts were undoubtedly more effective because of that. The Lord's words, "Be still and know that I am God" (D&C 101:16), became a living reality and a continual guiding influence. Fear of failure was replaced with confidence. I knew that the Lord would not let me fail, because the mission was His, not mine; the missionaries were His, not mine; the gospel is His, not mine. I am just an instrument in His hands.

I learned that when it comes to building the kingdom, I don't have to be the architect, builder, plumber, electrician, and landscaper. I don't have to do all these jobs. I only have one job and that is to trust in Him, take His hand, and do His will. Whether as a mission president, door greeter, home teacher, or father, that task remains the same. Our circumstances and challenges may differ, our sorrows and sufferings vary, but our need to focus on Christ is universal.

"Be of Good Cheer"

Shortly before His death, Jesus strengthened the disciples with teachings about comfort, peace, and joy. "These things I have spoken unto you, that in me ye might have peace," the Savior declared. "In the world ye shall have tribulation: but be of good cheer; I have overcome the world" (John 16:33). At first glance, the words *good cheer* and *peace* seem to be totally at odds with tribulation. In fact, they seem contradictory. How can I have "good cheer" amidst tribulation and trials? How can there be peace when I am up to my eyeballs in pains, problems, and pressures? The answer is found in the Savior's words "in me" and "I have overcome the world."

> Being of good cheer . . . is not naivete concerning conditions in the world—nor is it superficiality in reacting to the rigors of life. It is a deliberate, attitudinal and intellectual posture, a deep trust in God's unfolding purposes—not only for all mankind, but for each of us as individuals. Indeed, this attribute which Jesus spoke of might well be called "gospel gladness." It involves being constantly aware, and appreciative, of the ultimate justifications for our being of good cheer. Gospel gladness places the proximate frustrations and tribulations in needed perspective. If, however, our good cheer depends too much on the outcome of an election, or an athletic contest, or

having a good date, or on interest rates coming down, or the outcome of a sales contest, then our moods are too much at the mercy of men and circumstance. There are, to be sure, proximate things over which we can and should rightfully rejoice, but it is the ultimate things over which we can be of lasting good cheer. Note what Jesus said to the Twelve in this powerful scripture: "These things I have spoken unto you, that in me ye might have peace. In the world ye shall have tribulation: but be of good cheer; I have overcome the world." (John 16:33.) How was it possible for the Twelve to be of good cheer? The unimaginable agony of Gethsemane was about to descend upon Jesus; Judas' betrayal was imminent. Then would come Jesus' arrest and arraignment; the scattering of the Twelve like sheep; the awful scourging of the Savior; the unjust trial; the mob's shrill cry for Barabbas instead of Jesus; and the awful crucifixion on Calvary. What was there to be cheerful about? Just what Jesus said: He had overcome the world! The atonement was about to be a reality. The resurrection of all mankind was assured. Death was to be done away with—Satan had failed to stop the atonement. These are the fundamental facts. These are the resplendent realities over which we are to be of good cheer, even in the midst of the disappointments of the day. [We all need] to focus on these basic things which are firmly and irrevocably in place. Then [we] can better cope with the frustrations and tactical tribulations of the moment (Neal A. Maxwell, "But a Few Days," 4).

Having "good cheer" because of Christ's atoning victory over death and hell—over temptation, tribulation, sin, suffering, sorrow, weaknesses, inadequacies, and all the effects of the Fall—is faith-inspired confidence in the future. Like knowing the end from the beginning, we can rest assured that God and goodness will ultimately prevail. That "good cheer" evokes "things will all work out" optimism.

I am a huge sports fan. As my children would attest, I can really get into it. Unfortunately, that is not always good. If my team is locked in a tense, tight struggle, my stomach churns, my hands sweat, and my heart pounds. Instead of merely being entertained, I vicariously experience—both positively and negatively—"the thrill of victory, and the agony of defeat." Watching a game is like riding a roller coaster. There are moments of exhilaration and excitement, followed by panic and desperation.

It is interesting, however, that when I watch the video replay of my team's victory, I am much more calm and confident. Even if the quarterback throws an interception at a terribly inopportune moment or the opposing team scores a touchdown, I can sit back and enjoy the game because I know the outcome. I know that "things will all work out." (When my team loses, I don't watch the replays! I can't afford to relive the agony of defeat. There's a lesson in that as well.)

In the first chapter of this book, I shared with you the story of Peter walking on water, sinking in fear, and then catching hold of the rescuing hand of the Lord. I likened that to my own experiences. Just as Peter knew that he would not drown once he grabbed on to the Master, so too can we go forward with "gospel gladness" and "good cheer" confidence. For me, I don't know how far I still have to go to "get back in the boat." I don't know what tempests await, what waves and storms of life yet will crash against me. But like Peter, I have felt the rescuing hand of the Lord. Hand in hand with Him, I know I can make it—"so come what may" ("I Believe in Christ," *Hymns,* no. 134).

"Thank You for Extending Me Mercy"

There was a point in our mission that I wasn't sure I was going to make it—spiritually, physically, or emotionally. As one of the other mission presidents in our area observed, "This job can kill you." There was a turning point, however, that came in one of my darkest hours. It was a memorable and comforting moment, even at the time. Yet it is with 20/20 hindsight that I now can see how one simple act helped me to focus on Christ and allowed Him to strengthen me when I needed it most.

At the conclusion of our annual area mission presidents and wives seminar, we attended a temple session in the Winter Quarters Temple. Elder Dieter F. Uchtdorf and his wonderful wife, Harriet, had been with us throughout our conference. They had counseled us, instructed us, loved us, and strengthened us. There had been a remarkable spirit attending our meetings. I desperately needed that additional dose of love and support at that time.

But something else that Elder Uchtdorf did had an even greater impact on me. As we completed the endowment session and passed through the veil into the celestial room of the temple, Elder Uchtdorf greeted each mission president individually with a warm embrace and the words, "I love you."

I'm not sure that President Uchtdorf even remembers doing this, but I will never forget it. It may not have been a big deal to him or the others, but it was a monumentally transforming moment for me. I felt the love of the Savior emanating from this special witness into my soul. It was as if I was being embraced by the Lord Himself. That hug and the words "I love you" comforted and strengthened me more at that moment than all the training, teaching, and testimonies in the meetings.

I left that conference determined to share that feeling with my missionaries. I tried to follow the example of Elder Uchtdorf. We took every departing group of missionaries, on their last day in the mission, to the Nauvoo Temple for an endowment session. As Elder Uchtdorf had done with me, I greeted each missionary as they came into the celestial room at the end of the session with a big hug and the words, "I love you."

I expressed my appreciation for their service and friendship. I told them I was proud of them for faithfully fulfilling their mission. I meant every word of it, but, I must admit, it was easier to express those sentiments to some missionaries than others. We were very sad to say good-bye to some, and glad for others to go.

One elder in particular had given me more than his share of grief. In fact, many of the gray hairs that came after I was a mission president can be attributed to him. He seemed to be in trouble all the time. On more than one occasion, I told him that I was going to send him home. Yet he would always promise me that he would try harder. His renewed commitment didn't always last long, however. It certainly would have been easier for me, and perhaps better for the mission, to have just sent him home. Yet I could see some of me in him, and I wanted to see him succeed. I wanted him to be able to "return with honor." He wasn't an "all-star," but he made it.

As he came through the veil, I greeted him with the customary hug and "I love you." Tears streamed down his face. "Thank you for extending me mercy," he whispered as his whole body shook with weeping. It was a very tender moment and I, too, shed many tears. Almost as if the veil parted, I sensed a coming day when I would embrace the Savior and with tears of gratitude and love say, "Thank you for extending me mercy."

I am grateful that He has rescued me, not only from physical death and from sins, but also from myself—my fears, my discouragement, my doubts, my feelings of inadequacy. I am thankful that He is so long-suffering, as well. He never tires. He never fails. He never falters. He never gives up on me. He is always reaching out His hand to me and "running to" my rescue. Because of that, I am a different person—stronger, more confident, more full of faith, and more grateful for God's goodness.

I marvel that he would descend from his throne divine
To rescue a soul so rebellious and proud as mine,
That he should extend his great love unto such as I,
Sufficient to own, to redeem, and to justify.

Oh, it is wonderful that he should care for me
Enough to die for me!
Oh, it is wonderful, wonderful to me!

—"I Stand All Amazed," *Hymns,* no. 193

I bear testimony of the divinity of Jesus Christ and of His strengthening hand—the peace-giving, confidence-building, love-infusing, and joy-filling power of His atoning sacrifice for us. May you always keep your eyes focused on Christ—never looking beyond the mark or seeking that which cannot save or satisfy. May you learn to let Him heal you, lift you, carry you, and strengthen you. May you take hold of His outstretched hand and never let go.

I do not boast in my own strength, nor in my own wisdom; but behold, my joy is full, yea, my heart is brim with joy, and I will rejoice in my God.

Yea, I know that I am nothing; as to my strength I am weak; therefore I will not boast of myself, but I will boast of my God, for in his strength I can do all things.

—Alma 26:11–12

WORKS CITED

Bell, James P. "An Apostolic Call," *Brigham Young Magazine*, August 1994, 23–25.

Benson, Ezra Taft. *The Teachings of Ezra Taft Benson*. Salt Lake City: Bookcraft, 1988.

———. *A Witness and a Warning*. Salt Lake City: Deseret Book, 1988.

Collected Discourses Delivered by President Wilford Woodruff, His Two Counselors, the Twelve Apostles, and Others. Compiled by Brian Stuy. 5 vols. Sandy, Utah: B.H.S. Publishing, 1987–92.

Faust, James E. "Gratitude As a Saving Principle," *Ensign*, May 1990, 85–87.

Hafen, Bruce C. *A Disciple's Life: The Biography of Neal A. Maxwell*. Salt Lake City: Deseret Book, 2002.

"High School Runner Breaks Leg in Meet, Crawls to Finish Anyway," espn.com, accessed November 15, 2007.

Hinckley, Gordon B. *Teachings of Gordon B. Hinckley*. Salt Lake City: Deseret Book, 1997.

Holland, Jeffrey R. "Come unto Me," *Ensign*, April 1998, 16–23.

———. *Trusting Jesus*. Salt Lake City: Deseret Book, 2003.

Hunter, Howard W. "Conference Time," *Ensign*, November 1981, 12–13.

Hymns of The Church of Jesus Christ of Latter-day Saints. Salt Lake City: The Church of Jesus Christ of Latter-day Saints, 1985.

Kimball, Spencer W. *Faith Precedes the Miracle.* Salt Lake City: Deseret Book, 1972.

———. "Small Acts of Service," *Ensign,* December 1974, 2–7.

———. *The Teachings of Spencer W. Kimball.* Ed. by Edward L. Kimball. Salt Lake City: Bookcraft, 1982.

Lee, Harold B. *The Teachings of Harold B. Lee.* Ed. by Clyde J. Williams. Salt Lake City: Bookcraft, 1996.

Lewis, C. S. *A Grief Observed.* New York: Bantam Books, 1961.

———. *Mere Christianity.* New York: HarperCollins, 2001.

———. *The Problem of Pain.* New York: Macmillan, 1962.

Maxwell, Neal A. *All These Things Shall Give Thee Experience.* Salt Lake City: Deseret Book, 1980.

———. "But a Few Days." Address delivered to religious educators. Salt Lake City: The Church of Jesus Christ of Latter-day Saints, 1983.

———. "Meek and Lowly." In *Brigham Young University 1986–87 Devotional and Fireside Speeches.* Provo, Utah: University Publications, 1987, 52–63.

———. "Willing to Submit," *Ensign,* May 1985, 70–73.

———. *The Neal A. Maxwell Quotebook.* Compiled by Cory H. Maxwell. Salt Lake City: Bookcraft, 1997.

McConkie, Joseph Fielding. *The Bruce R. McConkie Story: Reflections of a Son.* Salt Lake City: Deseret Book, 2003.

Nelson, Russell M. "Divine Love," *Ensign,* February 2003, 20–25.

Oaks, Dallin H. *Pure in Heart.* Salt Lake City: Bookcraft, 1988.

Olsen, Andrew D. *The Price We Paid.* Salt Lake City: Deseret Book, 2007.

Packer, Boyd K. New Mission Presidents Seminar, Missionary Training Center, June 1998.

———. *"Let Not Your Heart Be Troubled."* Salt Lake City: Bookcraft, 1991.

———. *"That All May Be Edified."* Salt Lake City: Bookcraft, 1982.

Preach My Gospel. Salt Lake City: The Church of Jesus Christ of Latter-day Saints, 2004.

Scott, Richard G. *Finding Peace, Happiness, and Joy.* Salt Lake City: Deseret Book, 2007.

———. "We Love You—Please Come Back," *Ensign*, May 1986, 10–12.

Smith, Joseph. *Lectures on Faith.* Salt Lake City: Deseret Book, 1985.

———. *Teachings of the Prophet Joseph Smith.* Selected by Joseph Fielding Smith. Salt Lake City: Deseret Book, 1938.

Smith, Joseph F. *Gospel Doctrine.* Salt Lake City: Deseret Book, 1939.

Smith, Joseph Fielding. *Doctrines of Salvation.* Compiled by Bruce R. McConkie. 3 vols. Salt Lake City: Bookcraft, 1954–56.

Topliff, Vicki Bean. *Willard Bean, the Fighting Parson: The Rebirth of Mormonism in Palmyra.* N.p., 1981.

Widtsoe, John A. Conference Report, April 1922, 94–98.

Young, Brigham. In *Deseret News Weekly,* August 31, 1854, 37.

INDEX

"Abide with Me!" 19

Ambulance, 84–85

Atonement: entertaining self-punishing thoughts and, 30–34; scripture study and, 77–78; Jesus Christ's understanding and, 122–24; good cheer and, 130–31

Bean, Willard and Rebecca, 66–70

"Because I Have Been Given Much," 52

Belief, recognizing extent of, 93

Benson, Ezra Taft: on scripture study, 77–78; on general conference, 81

Best, doing your, 118

"Be Still, My Soul," 18

Blessings: author's father shows gratitude for, 35–37; missionaries express gratitude for, 40–41; from expressing gratitude, 42; keeping journal for, 43–45; prayer of gratitude for, 45–47; rich in, 47–50; callings as, 62–65; C. S. Lewis on, 87–88

"Called to Serve," 23

Callings, 62–65

Cannon, George Q., on promises of Jesus Christ, 104

Car accident, 84–85

Children of God, service and, 65–70

Church of Jesus Christ of Latter-day Saints, service in, 62–65

College graduation, 71–72

"Come, Come, Ye Saints," 21

Comfort: scripture study brings, 74–79; in Jesus Christ, 121–25
Comfort zone, 10
Commandment, to learn, 71–73
Control, giving up, 93–94
Cookies, 63–64
"Count Your Blessings," 38–39, 42
"Count Your Blessings" journal, 43–45

Depression, healing from, 125–28
Disciple, 74
Drowning person, 115–16
Drugs, 126–28

Education. *See* Learning
Eli, 90–91
Elisha, 95–97
Enduring to the end, 110–18
Experience, learning through, 1–3

Faith, gratitude and, 39–41
Family, service within, 60–62
Father, shows gratitude, 35–37
Faust, James E.: on gratitude, 40; as example of service, 63–64
Faust, Ruth, as example of service, 63–64
Fear, trust and, 90–92
First Presidency, on hymns, 16

General authorities, as examples of service, 62–64
General conference, 79–84

Good cheer, 129–31
Graduation, 71–72
Gratitude: of author's father, 35–37; focusing on Jesus Christ through, 37–39; faith and salvation and, 39–41; daily, 41–43; keeping journal to express, 43–45; prayer of, 45–47; for blessings, 47–50

Healing process, 125–28
Hinckley, Gordon B.: on gratitude, 46; on missionaries and service, 56; on learning, 72–73; on benefits of learning, 73; on meditation, 88–89; on faith, 128
Holland, Jeffrey R.: on coming unto Christ, vi; leans on Jesus Christ in new calling, 8–9; on using sacrament to focus on Jesus Christ, 29–30; as example of service, 63–64; on trust in Jesus Christ, 92; testimony of, 107–8
Holland, Patricia: on purpose of trials, 10; as example of service, 63–64
Holy Ghost: sacrament and, 28; listening to, 87–89; medication and, 127–28
Hunter, Howard W.: shines Neal A. Maxwell's shoes, 57–58; on general conference, 80
Hymns, 16–24

"I Know That My Redeemer Lives," 20
Irrigation ditch, 14–15
"I Stand All Amazed," 134

"Jesus, the Very Thought of Thee," 18
Jesus Christ: Jeffrey R. Holland on coming unto, vi; helps Peter walk on water, 7–8, 10–11; will help us through trials, 7–10; focusing thoughts on, 13–16, 128–29; using music to focus thoughts on, 16–24; using prayer to focus thoughts on, 24–28; using sacrament to focus thoughts on, 28–30; banishing self-punishing thoughts to focus on, 30–34; using gratitude to focus on, 37–39; service helps us draw nearer to, 52; Rebecca Bean's vision of, 67–69; service and, 67–69; learning of, 73–74; trust in, 92–94; trust in power of, 94–98; trust in promises of, 98–104; trust in love of, 104–8; enduring to the end with, 110–18; finding strength through, 121–25; mercy of, 131–33
Journal, "Count Your Blessings," 43–45

Kimball, Spencer W., 43; on service, 53–54; on feeling discouraged, 74; on benefits of scripture study, 75
Kindness, random acts of, 57–60

"Lead, Kindly Light," 22–23
Learning: as purpose for trials, viii–ix; through experience, 1–3; through experiences as mission president, 3–8; as commandment, 71–73; of Jesus Christ, 73–74; through scripture study, 74–79; from prophets, 79–84; temple as place of, 84–87; through Holy Ghost, 87–89
Lee, Harold B.: on conference, 82; on teaching doctrine, 125
Leg, broken, 109–10
Lehi, vision of, 111–13
Lewis, C. S.: on blessings, 87–88; on belief, 93; on being made perfect, 117
Life, requires focus, 15–16
Lifesaver, 115–16

Markwardt, Claire, 109–10
Marriage, of author's daughter, 49
Martin handcart company, 51–52
Maxwell, Neal A.: on purpose of trials, ix; on routine prayer, 24; Howard W. Hunter shines shoes of, 57–58; on enduring trials, 117–18; on Atonement, 123; on being of good cheer, 129–30
McConkie, Bruce R., on prophets, 81

McKay, David O., author's love for, 80

Medication, 126–28

Meditation, 87–89

Mercy, 131–33

Mesa Arizona Temple, 84–85

Micah's Cave, 22–23

Ministry, personal and private, 62–65

Mission president: author's trials as, 3–8; prayer helps author during calling as, 27; author banishes self-punishing thoughts as, 30–34; author assigns blessing journal as, 44–45; author's experiences with service as, 54–56; author learns importance of service as, 58–59; author learns power of scripture study as, 76–78; author learns to trust Christ's promises as, 103–4

Money, showing gratitude through, 35–37

Mother, missionary grieves for, 114–15

Music, 16–24

Nauvoo Illinois Temple, 49

Nub, 122–23

Oaks, Dallin H., on service, 53

Ochs, Nola, 71

Optimism, 119–21, 129–31

Packer, Boyd K.: blesses author, 4, 103; on controlling thoughts, 14–15, 31; on power of hymns, 17

Palmyra, New York, 66–70

Paul, 119–21

Perfection, 117–18

Perspective, 86–87

Peter, 7–8, 10–11

Pioneers, 21

Power of Jesus Christ, 94–98

Prayer: focusing thoughts on Christ through, 24–28; of gratitude, 45–47

Prophets, learning from, 79–84

Race, Claire Markwardt finishes, 109–10

Random acts of kindness, 57–60

"Redeemer of Israel," 19–20

Repentance, 30–34

Revelation, 1

Rich in blessings, 47–50

Sacrament, 28–30

Salvation, gratitude and, 39–41

Scott, Jeanene, 43–44

Scott, Richard G.: on letting go of past sins, 31–32; gratitude journal and, 43; on prayers of gratitude, 46; testimony of, 82–83

Scriptures: learning from, 74–79; examples of Jesus Christ's power in, 97–98; promises

made in, 100–102; examples of
Jesus Christ's love in, 105–6;
examples of enduring in,
111–13

Service: Brigham Young on,
51–52; drawing nearer to Jesus
Christ through, 52; leads to
greater spirituality, 53–57;
random acts of kindness and,
57–60; within family, 60–62;
within Church, 62–65; God's
children and, 65–70

Shoes, 31–32, 57–58

Sin, self-punishing thoughts and,
30–34

"Smile, Darned You, Smile,"
119–20

Smith, Joseph: on revelation, 1; on
virtue of Jesus Christ, 33; on
God's love, 105

Smith, Joseph F., on gratitude, 47

Smith, Joseph Fielding, on
sacrament, 28

Snelgrove, Laird, 72

Spirituality: service leads to
greater, 53–57; scripture study
and, 74–79; medication and,
127–28

Stairs, 91

Stone, Susanna, on pioneer songs,
21

Strength: finding, in weakness,
119–21; through Jesus Christ,
121–25

Succor, 124

Sun, 99–100

"Sweet Hour of Prayer," 26

Talmage, James E., 67–69

Temple, learning from, 84–87

Test, student prays to put off
taking, 45–46

Testimony: of Richard G. Scott,
82–83; of Jeffrey R. Holland,
107–8

Thanksgiving, missionaries express
gratitude on, 40–41

"Thorn of the flesh," 119–21

Thoughts: controlling, 13–15;
using music to focus, 16–24;
using prayer to focus, 24–28;
using sacrament to focus,
28–30; banishing self-
punishing, 30–34

Tree of life, 111–13

Trials: purpose of, viii–ix; as
mission president, 3–8; leaning
on Jesus Christ through, 7–10;
enduring, 117–18; of Paul,
119–21; good cheer and,
129–31

Trust: fear and, 90–92; in Jesus
Christ, 92–94, 128–29; in
power of Jesus Christ, 94–98;
in promises of Jesus Christ,
98–104; in love of Jesus Christ,
104–8

Uchtdorf, Dieter F., 131–33

Vacuum cleaner, 90
Virtue, 33

Water, 14–15
Weakness, finding strength in,
119–21
"When Faith Endures," 19
"Where Can I Turn for Peace?,"
18–19
Whitney, Orson F., on purpose of
trials, viii–ix

Widtsoe, John A., on temple
work, 86, 87
Winter Quarters Nebraska
Temple, 131–33
Worship: gratitude and, 46;
temples as central part of, 86

Young, Brigham: on service,
51–52; on doing our best, 118